SILENT ASSERTIONS

WOMEN'S AGENCY IN JAMMU AND KASHMIR POLITICS

SILENT ASSERTIONS

WOMEN'S AGENCY IN JAMMU AND KASHMIR POLITICS

Vibhuti Ubbott | Rekha Chowdhary

Vitasta

Published by
Renu Kaul Verma
Vitasta Publishing Pvt Ltd
2/15, Ansari Road, Daryaganj
New Delhi – 110 002
info@vitastapublishing.com

ISBN 978-81-963329-1-4

First Edition 2023
MRP 595

Edited by Kanagam King
Cover and layout by Somesh Kumar Mishra
Printed by Vikas Computer and Printers

Dedicated
to the Women of Jammu and Kashmir

Contents

Preface *ix*

Visible in Folk and Invisible in History 1

Women and Social Setting 15

Gender Question and Political Consciousness among Women 35

Women and Power Politics 56

Women and Conflict Politics 100

Conflict Politics and Agency of Women 141

Women and Agitational Politics 178

Conclusion *201*

Epilogue *207*

References *213*

Index *223*

Preface

Even when the politics 'around' Jammu and Kashmir and politics 'in' Jammu and Kashmir remain much in focus, the gender dimension does not get much attention. If women are mentioned as part of a political project, they are seen in secondary roles – as 'outsiders' to the area of politics; as passive recipients of policy decisions; as victims of conflict situation and so on. That women themselves may be at the centre of politics or that they may be political actors in their own right – is a point not taken into consideration by most of the political analysts while referring to the politics of Jammu and Kashmir.

We have, however, sought to bring women to the centre of politics in this erstwhile state – be it the power politics, protest politics or conflict politics. We have also sought to explore the 'agency' of women in various situations where they apparently seem to be playing a dormant role. We have recorded as to how women coped in very adverse situations. Silently, but very firmly, they asserted their rights and emerged strongly out of the conflict situation.

However, the journey of women in politics is not very easy. Confronted by the entrenched patriarchies – they are faced with all kinds of impediments, handicaps and obstacles.

It is the paradox of women's presence in politics in Jammu and Kashmir that makes a very interesting study. While one can talk about the high level of political consciousness of women, especially in the context of conflict situation, one also meanwhile notices almost a complete male monopoly over leadership positions – be it the power politics or the conflict politics. Being quite visible in street demonstrations or protest spaces, women have been seen as the face of mass politics. And yet, they are rarely to be seen in decision-making roles or holding leadership positions.

The book focuses on the role of women in various dimensions of politics of Jammu and Kashmir and seeks to link this role with the larger question of women. Noticing the absence of women's politics or a women's collective, it makes a case for reorientation of this politics from the gender perspective.

Visible in Folk and Invisible in History

While gender research has fully evolved in most places in India, in Jammu and Kashmir, there is a definite lag in this area. Not much attention has been paid to gender issues here. For one, research with respect to this state has been dominated by the context of conflict and issues emerging out of this context. This has been more so during the last three decades when the ongoing context of conflict came to be defined by armed militancy. Ironically, this has also been a period of intense research interest on Jammu and Kashmir, particularly on Kashmir, with a number of books, reports, documents and articles being published on the conflict situation. Despite the fact that the conflict situation impacted women in a variety of ways, the gender dimension generally remained severely underexplored. With the exception of a few isolated works on the impact of conflict on women, the concerns of women have generally remained marginalised.

To a large extent, such marginalisation is a legacy of the traditional societal bias against women in a male-dominated society. Inevitably, such a bias has also travelled in knowledge systems as well. There is not much literature available within the state which can help us trace the history from the perspective of women. Whatever historical accounts are available – mostly glorifying the feats of the rulers – do not depict the society from the perspective of women.

Explaining this point of marginalisation of women in the otherwise rich history of Kashmir, Krishna Misri, a prominent Kashmiri intellectual notes about the Kashmiri historiography, 'Selective women, measuring unto male standards, have been glorified, while others, who significantly impacted the Kashmiri ethos down the centuries, have been glossed over (Misri, 2010, 302).' She notes that:

> Going back in time, Pandit Kalhana's monumental work, *Rajatarangini* (1148-1149 AD), is the basis of historiography of Kashmir from primordial to his own times (1150 AD). The chronicle is focused on the succession of kings, conquests, treason, tyranny and murders followed by civil wars. Jonaraja updated the chronicle from 1150 to 1450 AD. However, the historiography attached little significance to women; hardly any historical documents chronicle the lives of Kashmiri women down the ages.
>
> (Misri, 2010, 305)

Misri narrates how the later versions of Kalhana's *Rajatarangini* written by Jonaraja and Pundit Shukla failed to refer to two most powerful women of Kashmir, namely Lal Ded and Habba Khatoon. These two women continue to have an impact on the day-to-day life of Kashmir, but they do not find mention in the *Rajatarangini* updated by later writers. To quote her,

> Surprisingly, Lal Ded… invoked by Kashmiris of all faiths in times of 'personal dilemma' does not figure in Jonaraja's *Rajatarangini*, though he updated Kalhana's famous chronicle and covered the historic period. Nor did Shrivara or Shuka, who succeeded him, mention her in their updated narratives.
>
> (Misri, 2010, 302)

About the prejudice against women in historical accounts, Asha Hans, a leading campaigner of women's rights (2000, 77-78), notes that it is the sexuality of women which gets noticed and not their administrative or political capabilities. To make her point, she refers to LN Dhar's essay, 'An Outline of the History of Kashmir' (Dhar, 1984, 1-28), where he has made mention of tenth century Hindu queen of Kashmir, Didda. He writes that Didda was a 'very unscrupulous and wilful lady' who 'led a very immoral life'. This point of her life seems to be emphasised over her capacity as an able ruler. Hans notes that 'women's power …is not perceived a power. Furthermore, universal sexual ethics are not applicable to women. Didda's sexuality is a barrier to her finding a place in history equal to male sovereigns of the period.' Hans further notes,

> Nationalist interests have perceived women as objects to be controlled. Nevertheless, we have to recognise that different historical understandings have produced different constructions of female roles. Dhar implies that Queen Didda transgressed the role circumscribed to females and, therefore, presents her as a target of contempt and ridicule. As the historiography of pre-independence years in India from a feminist point of view has yet to be explored, for a more authentic rendering, older histories would need to be examined… The exclusion of women from these shared memories of history influences women's place in the current nationalist discourse.

The folk, rather than the formal historical accounts, do more justice to women's role in the society. Lal Ded and Habba Khatoon are household names in contemporary Kashmiri society. It is the folk tradition that has carried their contributions from generation to generation. However, the popularity of these two women, as reflected in the folk, has failed to find appropriate appreciation in formal history.

Lal Ded or Lalleshwari is a woman who has a very strong influence on Kashmiri society. She is believed to be the spiritual teacher of Hazrat Noorani, the patron saint of Kashmir. Born in a Kashmiri Pandit family in the fourteenth century, she went through her personal journey of marriage and sufferings. Later, forsaking the material world, she emerged as a revered personality of Kashmir having sufficient influence on the generations to come. Her poetry, still popular among

Kashmiris, introduced a new vision for the common people to respond to the social, cultural and religious problems of the time. KN Dhar in his essay 'Lalleshwari: An Apostle of Human Values' notes,

> In her time, the friction between the past and present was acute; hence she, like an alchemist, by her healing touch, saved Kashmiri culture from being eroded and bruised. Her clarion call to assimilate human values in those dark days won for her the esteem and acclaim of Hindus and Muslims alike and the edge of ruthless proselytisation got blunted. It was no mean achievement on her part to unite the lost children of God, when every effort was being made to segregate them from one another. Her message was so universal and appealing that the tallest of Muslim Rishis of Kashmir, Sheikh Noor-ud-Din Noorani, made her his ideal.
>
> (Dhar, 1997, 68)

Ranjit Hoskote, the cultural theorist and art critic who has worked on Lal Ded, the famous Kashmiri poet, emphatically notes her (Lal Ded's) 'pervasive presence' in Kashmiri culture. What is significant about Lal Ded is that she is popular both among Muslims and Hindus. He says, 'It is true that Lal Ded was constructed differently by each community, but she was simultaneously Lallesvari [Lalleshwari] or Lalla Yogini to the Hindus and Lal'arifa to the Muslims' (Hoskote, 2013, 2).

Habba Khatoon was a poetess of the sixteenth century who rose from being an ordinary village girl to being the wife of Yousuf Shah Chak, the last autonomous King of Kashmir. As the story goes, Habba Khatoon was earlier married to a peasant and lived a life of misery. She expressed the ill-treatment by her in-laws in her verses. However, she caught the attention of Yousuf Shah Chak who got her divorced and married her. Later, when Yousuf Shah was exiled by the Mughals, she became an ascetic.

Known as the first modern poet of Kashmir, she 'gave the Kashmiri language a literary form and encouraged a synthesis of Persian and Indian musical styles'. She attained popularity through her verses in which 'she mocked the pretensions of the clergy, defended the mystic strain within Islam…' (Ali, 2002, 221).

One can see the same kind of gap between the folk and formal historical accounts of Jammu region. It is through the folk rather than the formal history that one gets insights into the Dogra society. Unlike Kashmir, which has a tradition of written history, Jammu does not have written history. It is only during the very recent period, particularly with the coming of the British to this part of the world, that some historical exercise was undertaken. And it is mainly with reference to legal initiatives taken by the Dogra rulers against the evil social practices against women like Sati, female infanticide, prostitution, etcetera that one can get some idea about the position of women.

There are a few popular folklores in the Dogra belt of Jammu region which depict the society from the perspective of women. In one of these folk stories, a newly wed woman is the central character who resists the objectification of women and their treatment as property of men. Recently, the story was reintroduced as *Ghumayee* by a local theatre group called

Natrang. It depicts the hard life of people in the treacherous hills and is woven around a small incident – that of uncontrollable thirst of a woman during her journey towards her new home. The indifference of the husband towards the wife and the sympathetic response by the poor carrier of the palanquin leads to an argument between the husband and the carrier, during which the husband pledges the wife to him if he succeeds in getting water for her. The carrier gets the water but dies after quenching the thirst of the bride. She thereafter refuses to go ahead with her wedded husband saying that she has become a widow because her husband had pledged her to the carrier. The story not only tells us about the nature of sufferings of women in a patriarchal society but also about the resistance of women. The fact that there is a temple attributed to this character in Udhampur district, also tells us about the way her resistance was acknowledged and respected by the society. Referring to some of these women who rebelled in one form or the other, London-based Dogra author Manu Khajuria mentions 'Bua Bhaga' whose Samadhi in Billawar tehsil is a testimony of her popularity after her death. 'She protested the unfair taxes imposed on the farmers by the *jagirdar* of Sumrata on the order of the raja of Bhaddu. Bua Bhaga opposed this taxation vehemently. She went door to door, carrying her newborn... urging people not to pay the taxes.' Besides this story, there are numerous popular Dogri folk songs that depict the loneliness and suffering of women left alone at the mercy of their in-laws. With the tradition of Dogra men earning their livelihood as soldiers and always at the 'service of the king' (*raje di naukri*), every second Dogri folk song describes the solitude of women.

Referring to the significance of the folk songs that represent the miseries and oppression of women, Vishav Raksha, a professor and author who specialises in gender and folk studies, thus notes:

> The Dogra are predominantly patriarchal and all the powers of decision-making lie with the men. Women are not able to express their feelings in open as they lack space for communication. Thus, they give expression to their feelings through folksongs and sing them in the absence of men. Although women have no power with them, but they are left with a lot of responsibility when the husband goes off to work in some other town or to serve in the army. The woman has to look after the house and family in the male's absence. This makes her tense and this tension is reflected in the folksongs.
>
> (Vishav Raksha, 2005, 219-221)

The oppression of women gets to be collectively acknowledged by the community through the peculiar concept of deities known as *Kuldevis* – commonly known as *Daati*. Manu Khajuria, mentions *Bua Amro* and *Bua Bhukht* who were oppressed during their lives but eulogised after their death; they were given the status of *Devi* and are worshipped on everyday basis in the shrines dedicated to them (Khajuria, 2018).

However, the historical accounts do not refer to women. According to historian Jigar Mohammad, if a reference is made to women, it is only to emphasise their secondary role in the society – their loyalty towards their husbands, their dependent nature and their sacrificing nature. Other than that, the history neither acknowledges the existence of women nor highlights their role and agency.

One may, however, mention some rare attempts to portray women in the social history of Kashmir. Prem Nath Bazaz's *Daughters of the Vitasta: A History of Kashmiri Women from Early Times to the Present Day (2011)* is one such attempt. There are also few books which locate women in the present socio-economic and political contexts. Bashir A Dabla has presented a sociological analysis of the problems faced by women in the changing social and political context of Kashmir. His three books *Multi-Dimensional Problems of Women in Kashmir* (2007), *Working Women in Kashmir* (1991), and *Domestic Violence against Women in the Kashmir Valley* (2009) were based upon empirical data. Aneesa Shafi's book, *Working Women in Kashmir: Problems and Prospects* (2002) deals with the issues related to women who have chosen to take up employment. Placing women in the changing scenario, the book analyses the contemporary woman's dilemma of managing the family and job at the same time. Another interesting book that provides an in-depth understanding of the situation of women in Kashmir's recent past is Sudha Koul's *The Tiger Ladies: A Memoir of Kashmir* (2002), which is in the form of a personal memoir.

However, in the last three decades, some literature has been made available that mainly seeks to understand the implications of conflict on women. Urvashi Butalia's *Speaking Peace: Women's Voices from Kashmir* (2002) seeks to represent various voices of women of Jammu and Kashmir. Containing the testimonies of ordinary women, it explores the implications of conflict from the perspective of women. Seema Kazi's *In Kashmir: Gender, Militarization, and the Modern Nation State* (2011) deals with the impact of militarisation and state violence on the women of Kashmir. It emphatically argues that militarisation does not lead to greater security for the state and also fails to provide justice for citizens. Inshah Malik's *Muslim Women, Agency and Resistance Politics: The Case of Kashmir* (2018) also deals with the impact of militarisation in Kashmir on women. The book however goes beyond the discourse of victimisation of women and focuses on agency of women in resistance politics. Nyla Ali Khan's book *Islam, Women, and Violence in Kashmir Between India and Pakistan* (2009) confronts the paradoxical relationship between religion and politics in Kashmir and analyses the implication of this relationship on women. Arguing that the turmoil in Kashmir has eroded the ethos of Kashmiri culture, she highlights the patriarchal nature of society and conflict politics and particularly focuses on adverse implications of the fundamentalist forces on the lives of Kashmiri women. Seema Shekhawat's *Gender, Conflict and Peace in Kashmir: Invisible Stakeholders* (2014) focuses on women's participation in the separatist politics of Kashmir. She raises concerns not only about the absence of women's voices but also their absence in leadership positions. Suneethi Bakhshi's *Kashmir: The History and Pandit Women's Struggle for Identity* (2009) focuses on the Kashmiri Pandit community that faced displacement due to the conflict situation. With a specific focus on women of this community, the book not only deals with their contemporary struggle vis-à-vis their cultural and gender identity, but also goes back in history to explore the question of their heritage and community identity. Another book that deals with the implications of displacement of the Kashmiri Pandit community on the women is *Conflict and Displacement in Jammu and Kashmir: The Gender Dimension* (2006) authored by Seema Shekhawat. Nayeema Mahjoor's *Lost in Terror* (2016) is an autobiographical account of the conflict situation from the gender perspective. There is also a biographical book on Begum Akbar Jahan, *The Life of a Kashmiri Woman: Dialectic of Resistance and Accommodation* (2014), by Nyla Ali Khan. Other studies focusing on gender context in conflict situation include Charu Walikhanna's *Women: Silent Victims in Armed Conflict* (2004), and *Women's Testimonies from Kashmir: The Green of the Valley is Khaki* (1994) by Women's Initiative.

However, notwithstanding the books mentioned above, there remain a lot of gaps in the understanding of the situation in which women are placed, particularly in the context of their political role, participation and agency. Most of the studies, with the exception of a few, have only dealt with victimisation of women; they have neither sought to explore how women have been participating in the mainstream or separatist politics nor have they focused on the agency of women or their role as leaders.

There are multiple paradoxes in relation to women's place in the politics of Jammu and Kashmir. Women are the most visible faces of the conflict politics of Kashmir and are seen as the face of mass resistance politics; however, they do not count at all within the decision-making positions. The separatist politics has been, in fact, a reflection of the patriarchal society in which gender difference is strictly followed, especially in the context of organisational roles and leadership positions. Mainly a male bastion, this politics clearly represented a continuity of the mainstream politics where women are almost invisible beyond the minimal level of voting. There is a huge gap between men and women when it comes to positions of power. This reality is pervasive throughout Kashmir, and in Jammu region also, there remains a huge paucity of women as decision makers – whether as political leaders, as contestants or members of Legislature. While much of Jammu's politics has been agitational, and women have been asserting their presence in large numbers, however, there is no women's autonomous politics.

The women's movements which overtook the rest of India during the 1970s and 1980s bypassed Jammu and Kashmir. And even when women have been participating in resistance and agitational politics, they have not been able to use their agency for their gender empowerment. The gender identity in any case is quite subordinated to the 'national', 'regional' and 'community' identity, and therefore the question of women's empowerment is the least significant question here. Women's politicisation is limited to their larger political identity assertions and not for the assertion of their identity as women. Despite the commonly shared problems of women across different parts of Jammu and Kashmir and across different community/ regional situations, there is no common women's politics. This explains why instead of sharing their gender perspective, they are utterly divided on the basis of their larger political identity.

The issue of political identity is the most potent one in Jammu and Kashmir. Here, the identity politics takes multiple directions. Besides the regional identity politics, there are various other identity politics that are constantly at play here. The multiple identity politics operate within the larger context of conflict which in itself is intricate and multi-layered. The book therefore seeks to locate women in the different dimensions of politics. Thus it seeks to explore their situation within the mainstream politics – agitational politics as well as separatist politics.

One of the major focuses of this study is on women's agency, especially in the context of the conflict situation. Though the victimisation of women remains a reality in the conflict situation, emphasis on victimisation does not provide a comprehensive understanding about women in conflict-ridden Kashmir. The assumption that men are responsible for the conflict situation and women are its passive recipients and are caught in this situation involuntarily, not only denies agency to women but also portrays them as 'apolitical' members of society. Women in Kashmir are not mute recipients but have been active political persons who have reflected various dimensions of their agency. Not only is their sense of identification with the conflict politics strong, they have furthermore been participating in this politics in a variety of ways. They have also been able to assert their cultural and gender identity in the context of the pressure coming from fundamentalist and revivalist forces. There are many examples of women silently but forcefully taking a position, both individually as well as collectively.

All this makes the study of women and politics in Jammu and Kashmir very interesting. Going beyond the perspective of victimhood, it is significant to know how women have coped with the complex consequences of conflict and how they have survived. Also important would be to know as to why, despite the fact that women had been quite involved in the separatist politics in the post-1989 period, they were not central to decision making and the peace process. Why there is almost no visibility of women in the dialogues, negotiations and other formal processes of peace building, remains the moot question related to women and conflict politics in Jammu and Kashmir. Despite the fact that women's victimisation formed the core issue of separatist politics, why did the gender context of women and women's issues not form the core of the conflict politics discourse? These are some important questions that this book seeks to address.

While focusing on the full range of politics in Jammu and Kashmir, the book seeks to explore the position of women in this politics. Tracing the history of the gender question in Jammu and Kashmir, it also seeks to analyse the absence of women in positions of power and decision making. More significantly, it seeks to locate the question of gender identity within the larger debate of larger ethnic/regional political identities. Simultaneously, it seeks to locate the agency of women, especially in the conflict politics.

Women and Social Setting

Though represented as a homogenous society, Jammu and Kashmir (whether as the princely state in pre-1947 period or one of the Indian states in the post-1947 period) has been quite plural, having multiple layers of diversity. Apart from religious diversity, this state also has linguistic, cultural, tribal and caste-based diversity. Broadly, the state was divided into three cultural zones – the Dogra zone, the Kashmiri zone and the Ladakhi zone. However, these zones did not in any case exhaust all the cultural variations within this erstwhile state. Though the Dogras (Hindus as well as Muslims) were the prominent community in Jammu region, this region was quite plural and besides the Dogras, it was a home to the Paharis, Gujjars, Kishtwaris, Bhaderwahis, and various other cultural groupings. Similarly, though Kashmir region was the most homogenous region with mostly the Kashmiri speaking people inhabiting it, even so, there were the Paharis and the Gujjars at the fringes of the Valley. Ladakh, the third region of the state was in itself a unique region, further representing the plurality and diversity of the society of this erstwhile state.

Being a plural society with multiple patterns of social diversity, the position of women within Jammu and Kashmir reflected multiple formats. Though, as elsewhere in the Indian sub-continent, the overall position of women was characterised by the patriarchal norms, however, there were a lot of internal variations. The social set-up of the Dogra society, dominated by the warrior classes, mostly the Rajputs, was quite different from that of the Kashmiri society, comprised of the peasantry and artisan classes. Within the Dogra and Kashmiri society also, there were different patterns characterised by class, caste, or tribal status. There were differences in the role and status of women depending on whether they belonged to the elite or the marginal sections of society. There were different ways of positioning women among some of the marginal groups and communities, including the Gujjars, Paharis and Dalits. Ladakh had its own peculiarities, and within this tribal society, there were further intricate differences on the basis of religious, sectional and class differences.

Historically, both in Jammu as well as in Kashmir region, the women in the upper crusts of society faced severe implications of patriarchal norms. Thus *purdah* (veil) was much more prevalent among the Dogra Rajputs and Kashmiri Muslim elite as compared to the lower castes and classes. Whether in Jammu hills or the fertile valley of Kashmir, the peasant women were working in the fields and therefore were not veiled at all.

With reference to the Kashmiri women, Farooq Ahmad

Bhat notes in his thesis on 'Kashmir Society as Reflected in Folk Literature: 1819 to 1947' that, here 'only the women of few privileged and orthodox Muslim families observed purdah in the strict sense of the term.' These aristocratic families, 'not to talk in public, even within the four walls of their houses… maintained separate chambers' for their women (Bhat, 2015, 269). Compared to them, the women who were part of the agrarian society or were associated with trading or cottage industry, never adopted veiling and had been granted a lot of freedom. It is a different matter however that these women, despite contributing a lot to the work and income in the house, had negligible control over the resources and property (Lawrence, 1895).[1]

Similar distinctions could be seen in other parts of the state. In Jammu region, the Dogra Rajput women who represented the upper crust of society were similarly 'protected' and veiled. As elsewhere in northern India, there was an inverse relationship between the caste status and gender status. Higher the caste of women, more were the restrictions on their movement. One can give the example of Mian Rajput women who were not allowed to visit even their parental family after they were married. As Frederick Drew, an English geologist who is noted for his geographical study of Kashmir, notes, a girl married at

1 Walter Roper Lawrence (1857-1940) was an English author who served in the Indian Civil Service in British India and was appointed as Settlement Commissioner for Jammu and Kashmir. While working on Settlement, he wrote travelogues covering the history, geography, flora and fauna, races, tribes, culture, society and people of Jammu and Kashmir.

the age of six to eight years, in a Mian family, 'never again returns to her family' (Drew, 1980, 51).

The caste and class context therefore mattered a lot in characterising the status of women. The freedom of mobility as well as the work status of women was linked with the class that they belonged to. Across the religious, regional and tribal divide, the women from lower classes were part of the work force and had relatively more freedom of mobility than women of the aristocratic classes. In Jammu region, the Dalit women were part of the work force along with men. In rural areas, they were seen working in the fields. The Gujjar women similarly were engaged in different kinds of work, including the production and marketing of goods, and therefore were not confined to the four walls of the house and were more mobile than the upper caste women. In Kashmir, the peasant women worked along with men in the farms, and the craftswomen similarly were involved in the making of handicraft goods. They were an important part of the shawl industry. To quote Bodha and Sheikh,

> ...the women used to engage themselves in shawl weaving, spinning of pushm and wool, weaving of blankets and putto manufacturing at their homes. Raw pushm was given to the women, who spun it into a [red] different degree of finesse. They sold it to the shopkeepers in small quantities, from whom it was brought by *karkhandars* (traders). The quality of shawl depended upon the dexterity and skill of the spinning. The wives of *Hanjis* (boatmen) engaged themselves in fishing in rivers and selling of fishes.
>
> (Bodha and Sheikh, 2017, 43)

Like the rest of northern India, the patriarchal norms were quite strictly followed throughout Jammu and Kashmir and there was a clear preference for boys over girls. The tradition of female infanticide was very common in the Dogra belt, and the Dogra state had to take legal steps to enforce its abolition. Again, the practice of female infanticide was more common among the elite and aristocratic classes; these included the Mians, Manhas, Salahria, Jamwal and Charak Rajputs (Sharma and Rana, 2015, 9). It was only after the British intervention that the local rulers took the initiative to stop this practice. To quote Drew,

> In the year 1846, much was done by the British representatives persuading the natives of chief rank and influence to agree together to exert that influence among their own people … and to lead by the example of their own families. Maharaja Gulab Singh joined in this movement hastily, and did much towards putting down the practice in his own country.
>
> (Drew, 1980, 50)

The dominant classes in the hill Dogra region were also involved in other patriarchal practices, including Sati and child marriage. Legal measures were later taken to stop these practices.

On the whole, the erstwhile state represented a varied and complex picture with respect to women. The traditions and social norms in each of the three regions varied. While the plains of Jammu were impacted by north Indian social practices; the Kashmir valley was insulated from the influence of northern India. Ladakh on its part was much more linked with Tibet and Central Asia and had its own peculiarities. Due to the paucity of land, there was prevalence of fraternal polyandry with two or more brothers marrying a single woman (Mann, 1978).[2]

It is true that some of the oppressive practices of northern India were not visible in Kashmiri society. For instance, there was no occurrence of female infanticide in Kashmir region. Similarly, there were no cases of dowry deaths. It is only recently that cases of female infanticide and dowry deaths have been reported. Making a case of Kashmir being an exceptional area, Ather Zia (2007), refers to the 'benign patriarchal norms of the Kashmiri society. Compared to much of the north Indian social set-up, here one does not find the kind of structured oppression that women were faced with. The narratives of female infanticide or widow oppression are absent here.'

However, even when women did not suffer the worst kinds of oppression, their position was not in any way equal to that of men. They were lagging far behind the men and did not enjoy the privileges and opportunities availed by men. Quoting Shamla Mufti, who rose to be the Principal of various girls' colleges in Srinagar, Sumona DasGupta, a political analyst and peace activist, who has worked in the area of women, conflict and security as a scholar-practitioner for three decades, notes that,

2 Prof. RS Mann (1936-2013), a well-known anthropologist, has worked extensively among various tribal as well as non-tribal communities of India. He has published extensively in the fields of ethnology, social and cultural change and anthropology, both theoretical and applied.

> Before 1947 the condition of Kashmiri Muslim women was one of complete suppression. There was stiff opposition to sending girls to school, general illiteracy was common among women, the hold of the orthodox *ulma* was strong, purdah was strictly observed in upper and middle class families. Girls were shut up within the four walls of the house and married off at puberty to anyone selected by their guardian. Psychologically trained to involve themselves only in household chores, they spent the day cooking and cleaning with social interaction confined to the premises of the home.
>
> (DasGupta, 2001, 21)

Though the system of prostitution was prevalent both in Jammu as well as in Kashmir, it was quite systematic in Kashmir and prostitutes were registered and taxed. There were two major centres of prostitution in Srinagar from where the prostitutes known as *Gaan* operated (Bodha and Sheikh, 2017, 43). As noted by many historians, the sale of girls as prostitutes was registered on stamp paper. Prostitution was also instituted in Jammu region, and the present Rajinder Bazar was known as the locality of prostitutes in those days (Sharma and Rana, 2015, 14).

On the whole, the position of women in Jammu and Kashmir in the pre-1947 period was defined by strict patriarchal codes. The women were not only excluded from basic resources for their own development, but they also faced severe oppressive norms, many of these being systematic and structural. As already stated, the Jammu and Kashmir state sought to bring about changes in these oppressive structures by initiating legal reforms and criminalising some of the social practices including those related to female infanticide, child marriage, widow remarriage and Sati. Some of these reforms started taking place during the time of Maharaja Gulab Singh, but the more systematic effort was made during the time of Ranbir Singh and later during the reign of Hari Singh. In 1928, Infant Marriages Prevention Act was adopted, and the minimum age for marriage of girls and boys was fixed at fourteen and eighteen respectively. It was during the same time that the Compulsory Primary Education Bill was passed (in 1930); state temples were thrown open for untouchables, Hindu Widows' Remarriage Act was passed and law was made against trafficking of women.

However, despite the legal changes, many of the negative practices continued even during the later period. The changes were quite difficult to bring about mainly because some of the practices that were sought to be abolished by law were deeply entrenched among the dominant ruling classes. So even when a proclamation was brought out by Maharaja Ranbir Singh to abolish Sati, on his own death in 1885, many of his wives committed Sati (Sharma, 2017, 220).

Notwithstanding the traditional peculiarities, modernity seems to have equally influenced all the regions of the state – allowing not only for opening up of opportunities for women, including those related to education and employment, but also in modernising the structures of patriarchy. In 1927, the Kashmiri Women's Welfare Association was established by GEC Wakefield. The initial members of the Association were mostly Englishmen. The Association had four sections dealing with educational, industrial, health and recreational activities. While the major activity of the Association was related to education, it also concerned itself with maternity and child welfare (Kaur, 1996, 61-62). Meanwhile, various social and religious organisations took upon themselves the responsibility of campaigning against some of the social evils, especially those related to women. The Arya Samaj, in this context, had established its branches in Jammu region during the beginning of the twentieth century – not just in Jammu town, but in various other towns of the region, including Mirpur, Kotli and Poonch belt. Later on, it could establish its branches in Srinagar town as well. As Kaur (1996) informs, it was the initiative taken by the Punjabis settled in the state who were initially influenced by the Arya Samaj movement. The Samaj was particularly concerned about some of the irrational social practices (Rai, 2004, 246-247).[3] Regarding the question of women, the goals of the Arya Samaj movement included those related to raising the status of women, abolishing the institution of child marriage, promoting widow remarriage and educating women (Kaur, 1996, 92-93). Meanwhile, among the Muslims of Kashmir, Anjuman-i-Nusrat-ul-Islam played

---

3 Mridu Rai is an Indian historian and author of the path-breaking work on Kashmir, *Hindu Rulers, Muslim Subjects: Islam, Rights, and the History of Kashmir.*

an important role in taking a lead in educational and social reforms. In Jammu, the Dogra Sadar Sabha was formed under the leadership of Lala Hans Raj; the Sabha had progressive goals including those relating to the upliftment and education of women.

The most important impetus towards change in the status of women was the introduction of education for them. Though it was during the time of Maharaja Pratap Singh that the idea of universal education was sown, it took root only during the time of Maharaja Hari Singh. It was under his regime that 'Compulsory Primary Education Regulation' was passed in 1930 and was made applicable in the major towns of the princely state, including Jammu and Srinagar (Khurshid, 2011, 40). By the first decade of the twentieth century, a number of primary schools, a few high schools and some colleges were established in the state. Beyond Jammu and Srinagar, women's education picked up in various smaller towns as well. Mirpur for instance had a good record of women's education before 1947. As Bal K Gupta (2011) notes in his memoir – a lot of women were educated in this town up to middle school which was the highest available education there. Of course men were educationally more exposed with many of them becoming high school graduates; and many could even go to colleges in Punjab and graduate there.

The first college (Sri Pratap College) was established in Srinagar in 1905 and in Jammu city in 1907 (Prince of Wales College). These colleges were open for both men and women and though these were predominantly attended by male students, a few female students were also part of these. However, in 1944, an exclusive women's college was started in Jammu (the Maharani Mahila College). It was in 1950 that a women's college was started in Srinagar city. The colleges contributed a lot towards popularising higher education among women in Jammu and Kashmir. How these exclusively women's colleges went a long way in expanding the horizons for women has been described by Krishna Misri in her description about Women's College Srinagar:

> The College catering to the educational needs of all segments of women soon became a symbol of their emancipation. Thousands of students who passed out of the college, year after year, were on a new trajectory. Many of them joined universities and professional colleges outside the state to acquire more skills and knowledge, and excelled in various fields. The increase in female enrolment over the years, in the professional institutions that the government opened, showed a positive trend.
>
> (Misri, 2010)

The establishment of women's colleges was in a way the first step towards developing a new kind of consciousness among women. To quote Farida Abdulla Khan, former Dean of Education at Jamia Millia Islamia, who has expertise on issues related to education in India and Kashmir,

> Colleges for women were set up by the state under a socialist program rather than by elite groups or philanthropic organizations with their own agenda for women's education. The goal was no longer to produce 'good' mothers and

> 'dutiful' wives, but partners in the development and progress of the region and its people, and the emergence of a 'new' Kashmir.
>
> (Khan, 2005, 136)

She noted that 'the establishment of Women's College was a reflection of the changing times.' With political demands being made to end the feudal order and abolish the monarchical structure, there was also a demand to empower the people in general. This helped in generating awareness about other problems of society and changing the attitudes towards women.

Education for women started increasing in the sixties and seventies and by the end of the eighties, the number of schools and colleges for women had increased manifold. Every district had one women's college and several higher secondary schools meant exclusively for women. Meanwhile, there have been increased opportunities for girls to avail higher education through various universities established in the state. Though initially there was only one university for the whole state of Jammu and Kashmir, gradually the number of universities has been increasing. At present, there are around nine or ten universities which include two older regional universities; two central universities located in each of the regions; two agricultural universities (one of each located in Jammu and Srinagar cities); and a few universities established by religious and charitable organisations (like Baba Ghulam Badshah University in Rajouri; Islamic University in Srinagar; Shri Mata Vaishno Devi University in Katra). The available data provided by *Digest of Statistics* of Jammu and Kashmir shows that women have grabbed the opportunity to be educated in colleges and universities. As per this data, the number of females getting educated in institutions of higher education exceeds that of male students. Situation is encouraging for professional colleges as well.

One can therefore see a notable change in the opportunities that women have been provided with especially in the urban areas. In the cities of Jammu and Srinagar and large towns like Anantnag, Baramulla, Sopore, Kathua, Udhampur, etcetera, women have not only been exposed to general education but also to professional education and employment opportunities. By the second and third decade after Accession, the number of women who were educated and were pursuing careers was increasing. The towns and cities became vibrant centres for girls' education. As DasGupta notes,

> By the 1960s a considerable number of women had come out of the purdah. School and college education became a routine matter and women entered new professions – as teachers, lecturers, doctors, lawyers, as well as the service sector. However, class and regional disparities continued. The new educational trends also had an impact on the pattern of marriages with the increasing demand for a working wife. The lack of a job was expected to be compensated by dowry creating new social pressures.
>
> (DasGupta 2001, 22)

University education especially became quite accessible for

women; one could see that both in Kashmir and Jammu cities, the universities have had high visibility of women students.[4]

The opening of educational institutions for women was a catalyst for various other changes in the lives of women. They could discover their own identity and look for opportunities other than those provided by the traditional society. Misri notes,

> Stepping out of the shadows of usual familial, caste and religious identities, they emerged with their own professional identities, in diverse fields of activity. The changing landscape saw them making their own small choices and this reflected in their dress, demeanour and deportment.
>
> (Misri, 2010, 311)

It was a reflection of the spread of education that Jammu and Kashmir could boast of a small group of women elite by the 1960s – mostly educated women belonging to the middle class and from the upper crust of society. Of these women, Mehmooda Ahmed Ali Shah, Shamla Mufti, Krishna Mohan, were educationists; there were others like Krishna Mehta who rose to be the first woman MP from Jammu and Kashmir; Padma Sachdev, a famous Dogri writer who became a leading cultural figure; and Shanta Bharati a social and political activist. By 1970s, medical profession had started opening up for women

---

4 The government data shows that the number of women seeking higher education has been consistently increasing. Thus, as against 61,399 women students enrolled in higher education in 2010-11, their number had increased to 1,03,195 by 2014-2015. (*Digest of Statistics*) The situation is as promising in professional education.

and as the government reserved substantial seats for them in the medical colleges of Jammu and Kashmir, a number of women doctors were trained. By the 1990s, women had started getting admitted in engineering colleges and were now getting trained in new professions like Information Technology, Management, Architecture and Law. Unfortunately, while some of the women trained in these professions took up a career in their respective fields, many others did not.

However, while women, at least some of them, were being exposed to new opportunities and getting into professional education and looking at new career opportunities, the society was reproducing the gender biases though in a more modern form. While making available opportunities to women, patriarchy was also getting reinforced, albeit in different forms.

Thus, while statistics of the post-1947 periods reflect a lot of change in the status of women, they also reflect the continuity of the discriminatory practices against women on the one hand and even extension of these practices in places where these did not exist on the other hand. Kashmiri society, which traditionally was not known for the practice of 'dowry' or for violence against women, has started showing these trends in the recent period (Dabla, 2014). Similarly, domestic violence against women has been on the increase – both in Kashmir and in Jammu region. As per the 2015 Crime Branch report of Jammu and Kashmir, there were 1247 cases of domestic violence registered in Jammu division and 439 cases in Kashmir division (Ladakh that was a part of the state at that time had only 4 cases) (*The Economic Times*, May 22, 2015).[5] On the whole, there was an increase in the crimes against women. As per the National Crime Records Bureau Report, in 2020, there were as many as 487 cases of attempt to murder. There were also 35 cases of abetment of suicide and 24 cases of abetment of suicide of women in 2020. The Report also suggests that though there were a few reported cases of dowry deaths, there were many reported cases of rapes (247),[6] and as many as 349 reported cases of cruelty against women by husbands or relatives. A number of cases of assault against women were also reported – these included 1,639 cases of assault on women and 1,744 cases of assault on women with intention to outrage their modesty (Yusuf, 2021).[7]

As far as the overall socio-economic profile of women in this erstwhile state is concerned, they suffer from many gender specific disabilities like low sex ratio, low work participation, lower health status, etcetera. They have been lagging in almost all the indices of growth and well-being. The Census of India 2011 recorded the sex-ratio in J&K at 889 (Census of India). The child sex ratio shows a further downward trend at 862. It is pertinent to mention here that the child sex ratio in J&K

5 As per the National Family Health Survey (NFHS) in 2019-2020, in the age group between 18-49, domestic violence was experienced by 9.6% women in J&K. The number of women facing domestic violence in the rural areas was still higher (11%). The NFHS data for sexual violence says that in 2019-20, 5% rural women in the age group of 18-29 have experienced sexual violence at the age of 18. For urban woman the percentage is lower (1.4%).

6 Report also mentions 30 cases of stalking that included 15 cases of sexual harassment.

7 Article in *Greater Kashmir* by Shabir Ibn Yusuf.

has recorded the sharpest decline of 8.4% since the last census, across all the states in India, which is an alarming situation. The health situation of women is not very promising.

> Anaemia... is a major health problem in Jammu and Kashmir, especially among women and children.... 40 percent of women in Jammu and Kashmir have anaemia, including 29 percent with mild anaemia, 11 percent with moderate anaemia, and 1 percent with severe anaemia.
>
> (NFHS-4,2016: P21)

As far as the work participation of men and women in Jammu and Kashmir is concerned, the situation is dominated by men – of the total work force here, men formed 81.35% and women formed only 18.65%. In this small percentage of women, a large percentage have been classified as marginal rather than main workers. As per the 2011 census data, of the total female workforce, 70% were marginal workers and only 30% were main workers. This is in contrast to male workers where 72% were the main workers and 28% the marginal workers.

Compared to men, women in Jammu and Kashmir have also been lagging as far as control over resources is concerned. Like anywhere else in India, women have been participating in the agricultural chores as much as or even more than men, however, they don't have much control over the land. The land generally is in the name of men. The NFHS survey (2016) gave us data which reflects the gap between men and women in this regard and notes that while 73% of men own land alone or jointly with someone else, only 27% women hold it. It also notes while 81% of men aged 15-49 own a house alone or jointly with someone else, only 33% of women of the same age own it. '42% of women have some money that they can decide how to use, 3/5th of women have a bank or savings account that they themselves use and only 47% of women are allowed to go by themselves to all three of the following places: the market, a health facility, and places outside the village/community (NFHS-4,2016: P27).' The survey also noted the lack of agency among a large number of women in relation to the major decision that affects the quality of their life. As per the NFHS data of 2020, '51% of women and 79% of men (15-49) own a house alone or jointly with someone else, and 51% of women and 70% of men own land alone or jointly with someone else. Among men and women, ownership of a house and land is more common in rural than urban areas. (*Kashmir Life*, 2022)' The position of women vis-à-vis employment continues to be bleak. Less than 30% women were employed and there was a vast gap between men and women's employment. The same survey revealed that a large number of women (10%) had experienced physical violence (including 3% who experienced sexual violence) and in many cases such violence is committed by their husbands. Worse, many of these women never sought any help, while only a small number (4%) sought help from the police. However, the most revealing aspect of the survey was that a large number of women (49%) stated that a husband is justified in using violence against women under some circumstances (*Kashmir Life*, 2022).

On the whole, one finds that though women's position has been improving as compared to what it was, say a century ago, yet, they continue to be governed by a number of disabilities. The paradox in the position of women gets very clear from the increased visibility of women in the educational field, especially in higher education, and yet, there are large number of women who continue to be illiterate. The educational policy of the state government which was quite liberal and was aimed at providing free education up to the university level, somehow did not reach the vast mass of rural people, especially the women.[8] Though in relative terms the span of education extended itself significantly compared to what it was before 1947, and a middle class was created, but still a large number of people were left out. And among those who were excluded, women formed a large number. As the literacy data of 2011 census suggests, as late as six decades after the Accession, 44% of women still fell into the category of illiterates. Compared to the male literacy rate of 76.75%, the female literacy rate was 56.43%. As per the data, in some of these districts, there was a very wide gap between male and female literacy. Besides the literacy data, the data on enrolment of girl students shows a

8 This gets clearly reflected from the latest data of literacy in the undivided state of Jammu and Kashmir. Here the rate of literacy (excluding 0-6 years) amongst females has been 56.43% as compared to 76.75% for males (Census of India-2011). What it effectively means is that as large a percent as 44% of the female population of the state was illiterate in 2011. The situation was certainly worse in some districts where the percentage of illiterates among the female population was still higher – thus 62% women in Ramban district, 58% women in Kishtwar, 56% in Bandipora and Budgam districts, 54% in Ganderbal, 50% in Shopian, Doda and Kupwara districts, 49% in Pulwama, and 48% in Anantnag were illiterate.

gap between male and female enrolment at all the levels, be it the primary schools, the secondary schools or the higher secondary schools.[9]

The paradox of women's social position also gets reflected in the visibility of women in various professional institutions and some limited visibility as professional careerists, women entrepreneurs, women administrators and police officers – and the great gap between men and women in most of these situations. Women have started entering the areas which earlier were mainly occupied by men and yet they continue to represent only a small minority.

9 As per the data provided by the *Statistical Digest* of Jammu and Kashmir, in 2016-2017 there were 3.96 lakh girls enrolled in the primary schools as against 4.23 lakh boys; in middle school 2.59 lakh girls as against 2.85 lakh boys and in the higher secondary schools, there were 2.60 lakh girls enrolled as against 3.02 lakh boys. The data also suggested that 'compared to 29 percent of men, less than one-fourth (22%) of women age 15-49 in Jammu and Kashmir have completed 12 or more years of schooling (NFHS-4,2016: P4).'

Gender Question and Political Consciousness among Women

Gender Question

Before posing the question of 'women' in public life and politics, it is important to explain the nature of the politics in Jammu and Kashmir and the implication that this politics has on women. Two prominent features of politics in this erstwhile state may be mentioned. First, due to the complex social diversity, the politics here also takes the plural form. The multiplicity of identity politics is therefore a prominent feature of the politics here. While Kashmiri identity politics remains the most visible form of this politics, there are other kinds of identity politics including Jammu's regional identity politics, sub-regional identity politics of Doda belt and the Poonch-Rajouri belt, tribal politics including that of the Gujjars and Paharis as well as the caste politics (Chowdhary, 2010). The second feature relates to the range of politics that stretches from the formal politics to the agitational and conflict politics. No study of women in politics will be complete if we do not refer to the multiplicity of identity politics and their location in all the three dimensions – formal-competitive, agitational and conflict politics. However, before we attempt an analysis of women and politics with respect to each of these forms of politics, it may be important to focus on the women's question – how has the women's question been addressed by this erstwhile state (and now the Union Territory) of Jammu and Kashmir.

The women's question along with the question of other marginal classes (including the peasants, craftspeople and workers) was an important one for the anti-feudal movement politics of Kashmir in pre-1947 period (Bazaz, 1954). Though initially this politics was organised around the religious identity of Kashmiris, gradually it started acquiring a progressive character. The year 1939 marked a watershed moment in Kashmir's politics when the All Jammu and Kashmir Muslim Conference was transformed into All Jammu and Kashmir National Conference. Under the influence of left intellectuals and the members of the Communist Party of India, the movement politics not only acquired mass character but also started catering to the interests of the common people. By 1944, this changed character of the movement politics was ideologically streamlined with the adoption of a manifesto titled *Naya Kashmir* (New Kashmir Manifesto). This Manifesto while elaborating on the vision of self-government, also detailed the future vision of the socio-economic structure of society. Accordingly, the Manifesto had three Charter of Rights – the Peasants' Charter, the Workers' Charter and the Women's Charter. The Women's Charter promised various rights to women. With the view that 'men and women must collaborate with each other in shouldering the weighty responsibility of nation building', this Charter made commitment in favour of universal suffrage for women above the age of eighteen years as well as the right of women to be elected in elected institutions. It also promised that all matters concerning women that are to be decided by the elected organs of the state were to be adopted after due consultation with the representatives of women. Among other commitments that were made by the Manifesto included those related to employment – similar wages for similar work; right to follow any trade or profession that women are capable of according to their will and consent; same social insurance scheme for women working in industries as available to men; special rights for antenatal and post-natal care and medical help; paid maternity leave for six months; baby care and kindergarten facility. Mention was also made about the social rights of women including legal protection to the status of women; protection from trafficking and prostitution and special care of women belonging to backward tribes and backward regions of the state. The Charter also provided for legal and educational rights of women. The legal rights included the right to choose husband according to a woman's will and discretion; abolition of dowry system; right to obtain divorce or separation; equal and humane treatment of women prisoners. The educational rights included compulsory and free education for all women; mobile schools for nomadic women and boat schools for boat-women; scholarships to women at all levels (All Jammu and Kashmir National Conference, 1944).

The commitments made in the New Kashmir Manifesto of the National Conference were later incorporated into the Constitution of the state. The Directive Principles incorporated into the Constitution of the state were much wider than those incorporated into the Constitution of India and the rights of women were an inherent part of these Directives. Section 22 specifically referred to the endeavour of the state to secure for all women a number of rights which included, most importantly, the right to equal pay for equal work; the right to full equality in all social, educational, political and legal matters. It also provided for the 'right to maternity benefits as well as adequate medical care in all employments' as well as 'the right to reasonable maintenance, extending to cases of married women who have been divorced and abandoned'. It also referred to 'special protection against discourtesy, defamation, hooliganism and other forms of misconduct'. Among other rights mentioned in the Constitution, there were certain universal rights granted to men as well as women. In some of these universal rights, specific mention of women was also made. Thus it was mentioned that 'all permanent residents, men and women equally, have the right to work, that is, the right to receive guaranteed work with payment for labour in accordance with its quantity and quality, subject to a basic minimum and maximum wage established by law'. In another reference to women, it stated that provisions should be made for ensuring 'that the health and strength of workers, men and women, and the tender age of children are not abused and that permanent residents are not forced by economic necessity to enter avocations unsuited to their sex, age or strength.' There were other universal rights in which there was no specific reference to women, but still in their scope, these applied to women. This included the directive for making a law to ensure 'that all permanent residents have adequate maintenance in old age as well as in the event of sickness, disablement unemployment and other cases of undeserved want by providing social insurance, medical aid, hospitals, sanatoria and health resorts at State expense'. The directive also stated that the state shall endeavour 'to secure for every permanent resident the right to free education up to the University standard; to provide, within a period of ten years from the commencement of this constitution, compulsory education for all children until they complete the age of fourteen years' (All Jammu and Kashmir National Conference, 1944).

Women's question, as we can see from an analysis of the New Kashmir Manifesto and the Constitution of Jammu and Kashmir, was an important question due to the very nature of politics of the 1940s and early 1950s. The political ideology of the National Conference, the major political organisation of Kashmir and later the erstwhile state of Jammu and Kashmir, had strong socio-economic content and that is the reason why the post-Accession policy framework of Jammu and Kashmir was quite progressive and people-oriented. However, as the state got entrapped into conflict politics in the post-1953 period, the progressive content of politics was completely side lined. In the next few decades, it was only the issue of the political identity of Kashmir that was privileged, and all the issues related to peasants, the socially purposive politics, was relegated to the background.

It was for this reason that women's movement politics that captured the nation's imagination in the seventies and eighties completely bypassed the erstwhile state of Jammu and Kashmir. While northern India was impacted by the Dalit movement, the women's movements, the right to information movements, Jammu and Kashmir remained totally untouched by these. The political identity question became so important that not only the politics of Kashmir was dominated by it, but the regional response of Jammu and Ladakh also came to be defined by it. While it was Kashmiri nationalism and Kashmiri political identity that was asserted in Kashmir, it was regional identity of Jammu and Ladakh that was asserted in these two regions. Despite the clear distinction in the nature of politics on regional basis, what remained common was the primacy of 'political identity' and 'political questions' over the socio-economic questions.

This was much more clear in Kashmir where there was continued political mobilisation in the post-1950 period. Here, Kashmiri identity became the central point underlying the political movement politics and all political mobilisation took place around this identity. The gender question was not raised and if anything, it was made subservient to the Kashmiri identity politics. By implication, the concerns of women were neither addressed nor were considered important. The progressive agenda that one could see in the New Kashmir Manifesto, no more dominated the Kashmiri politics. What was worse, the patriarchal trends in the Kashmiri identity politics remained totally unquestioned.

The patriarchal approach to the Kashmiri identity politics became quite visible around a very important question related to the domicile law of the state – a law related to the rights of the permanent residents of the state. As per this law, the permanent residents of the state were granted special privileges related to ownership of land; state government employment; state fellowship; admission in state run professional institutions; the right to vote and contest in State Panchayats and State's Legislative Assembly. However, as per the administrative practice, a distinction was made between male and female permanent residents of the state. The Permanent Residence Certificate (PRC) was generally stamped as 'valid till marriage' and in case a woman married a person from outside the state, she was no more considered a permanent resident of the state. Women like her could not get a fresh PRC and therefore were deprived of the privileges enjoyed by the the permanent residents. These privileges included the right to pursue employment in the state services; the right to hold property in their name; the right to vote for the state legislature and panchayats; and right to contest elections and hold any political office in the state. This was an administrative practice which was not supported by any provision of the State Constitution. It was only in 2002 that this practice was discontinued following a full bench decision by the J&K High Court in a case filed by Dr Sushila Sawhney and many others (State of Jammu and Kashmir …vs Dr Sushila Sawhney, 2002).

This verdict corrected the administrative anomaly which restricted the rights of women married outside the state. By a full bench, the High Court opined that the daughter of a permanent resident of J&K will not lose her status as a permanent resident if she marries a person who is not a permanent resident of the state. It stated that there is no provision in the existing law dealing with the status of a female permanent resident who marries a non-permanent resident.

This decision was considered historic because it pushed away a discriminatory practice and brought relief and equality to women. However, the discriminatory content of the law continued as women married outside the state could not transfer their property to their children (While the children of the males married outside the state enjoyed the full right to be considered as the permanent residents of the state, the children of females married outside the state were barred from being granted the PRC). But still there was a substantial relief to women marrying outside the state. A sense of justice and fairness prevailed in this decision. However, in Kashmir, there was not much of an enthusiastic response. Notwithstanding the discriminatory nature of the law, there remained a consensus in Kashmir valley in its favour. Any discussion around the need to change it was strongly resisted as it was seen to be endangering the 'Kashmiri identity'. An argument was developed that extending the right of permanent residence to women married outside the state or her children would amount to changing the demography of the state and endangering the 'Muslim majority character of the state'. This was a clear case of subordinating the gender rights and submerging the question of women in the larger question of 'political identity' of Kashmir.

Giving a representation to the views expressed in Kashmir, the then People's Democratic Party (PDP) led government sought to undo the High Court's judgement by filing a special leave petition in the Supreme Court. Later, it withdrew the judicial appeal but its law minister Muzaffar Hussain Beigh introduced the 'Jammu and Kashmir Permanent Resident Status (Disqualification) Bill 2004' in the state legislature. This bill got the full support of the National Conference and was unanimously passed in the Legislative Assembly in 2004. However, as it created a lot of controversy, it was stalled and could not be made into a law. The issue however remained alive with the PDP vociferously arguing that a law is required to disqualify women married outside the state. The Permanent Resident (Disqualification) Bill 2010, introduced in the Legislative Council by Murtaza Khan of the PDP, was an effort in this direction. This bill was later dropped due to a 'technical' flaw – since it pertained to a constitutional matter and it could not be initiated in the upper house of the legislature.

The bills, as introduced in 2004 and as resurrected in 2010, had been used to generate political emotions in Kashmir. It was argued that restrictions on women's rights are necessitated to preserve the political identity of Kashmir. The right of women to marry outside the state and retain their PR status was seen as contradictory to the autonomy and special status of the state. There was a campaign that such a right given to women would ultimately lead to a demographic change in the state. Fear was expressed that the right of women to hold their PR status even when they were married outside the state would open the floodgates to the non-permanent residents enabling them to swamp the state and control the property and employment in the state.[10] The concerns for protection and preservation of Kashmiri identity therefore overrode the concerns for women's rights.

However, it was not only in Kashmir that the gender identity was subordinated to the political identity of the community. Almost in a similar vein, the discourse in Jammu was also based on the lines of regional, communal and national identity. The bill to disqualify married women from holding the PR status was opposed not so much from the perspective of women's rights as on the ground that it was 'anti-Jammu', 'anti-national' and 'anti-Hindu'. The campaign against the bill, both within as well as outside the legislature, was carried out mainly by the radical forces whose major objection to the bill was its pro-Kashmir and anti-Jammu bias. Many Jammu-based parties and organisations found in the bill another instance of discrimination against Jammu. The bar association of Jammu actually called for a Jammu *bandh* (general strike) to agitate against the 'anti-Jammu' and 'anti-Hindu' nature of the bill.

10 The political class in Kashmir, across the party and ideological lines, whether belonging to the separatist or the mainstream politics, supported the disqualification of women in 2004 in the interest of, what was termed as, the preservation of Kashmiri identity. Nothing unusual was seen in the subordination of women's rights to Kashmiri identity. In 2010, too, the general refrain was that the bill does not concern women as much as it concerns the Kashmiri identity facing threats from external forces.

That women's question has not assumed much importance in Jammu and Kashmir is reflected in the fact that there are many crucial gender issues that remain unaddressed by the policy makers. One such issue which assumed critical dimensions is related to the depleting sex ratio. This issue needed the focus of the state, particularly after the 2011 census revealed an inverse trend since 2001. Despite the fact that the developments related to sex ratio have been alarming, there has neither been much of societal or state response. From 892 in 2001, the sex ratio went down to 883 in 2011. What was more alarming was that the sex ratio of girls up to the age of six was still lower than the overall sex ratio. For every one thousand male children, only 859 female children were reported (Chowdhary, 2015).

This kind of data should have generated a sense of crisis in the state mainly for the reason that the sex ratio had worsened between 2001-2011. In 2001, the child sex ratio for the state was 941 and was much above the national average of 927. However, in 2011, while the all-India child sex ratio was recorded at 914, for J&K, it had gone down to 859.[11]

The lowering of sex ratio is not the only issue related to women; there are issues related to crimes and violence against women which do not catch much attention. Much of this is

---

11 Situation was so bad for Child Sex Ratio that two of the districts of the state fell in the lowest ten districts in all-India count – Samba with CSR at 787 and Jammu with CSR at 795 – lowest district in the country being Jhajjar with CSR at 774. Further there were thirteen other districts of the state which were placed much below the national average. These included Anantnag, Badgam, Rajouri, Kupwara, Ganderbal, Baramulla, Srinagar, Kulgam, Shopian, Udampur and Bandipore.

a consequence of an absence of women's activism in the state. Moreover, in the conflict-ridden state, political identity questions assume importance over the gender identity question. This is why the major questions of gender rights are framed within the context of identity politics. Issues of sexual crimes are not seen from the perspective of women but from the perspective of its political context. Since conflict situation has aggravated competitive identity politics, there is sharpening of community identities. This has a clear implication for women's question.

That the response of the state towards women's question has been very casual gets reflected in the absence or long delays in providing the institutional mechanisms for dealing with their specific concerns. Thus it took a long time for the state to provide for one-third reservation for women in the Panchayats even after PRIs (Panchayati Raj Institutions) were constituted under the local Act of 1989. It was in 2001 that the Panchayat election took place under this Act and there was provision for nomination for women but no provision for one-third reserved seats for women. Later when the provision for women's one-third representation at the level of *panchs* was incorporated in 2004, the provision for reservation at the level of *sarpanchs* was not introduced. In the 2011 election therefore, one could see a dismal representation of women as *sarpanchs*, even when there was a large number of women *panchs*. The casual approach of the state could also be seen from the way the State Women's Commission has been handled. Except for the first five years of its functioning, the Women's Commission has for a larger period been a headless body.

Rise of Political Consciousness and Women

Jammu and Kashmir was one of those princely states which witnessed a strong movement politics. This politics was oriented against the feudal and monarchical system and was mainly located in the valley of Kashmir. Initiated in the decade of 1930s, this movement politics was limited to the middle class educated intelligentsia, but by 1940s, it had incorporated a large number of common people. The peasantry, the craftsmen, the working class and other Kashmiris had been mobilised in large numbers. The political movement had reached the grassroots level after the inception of the All Jammu and Kashmir National Conference.[12]

The National Conference being a mass organisation had its cadre up to the level of the villages. As already stated, it had launched the blueprint of its ideology in 1944, in the form of the New Kashmir Manifesto that incorporated the progressive pro-people ideology with a special focus on peasants, workers and women. Its mass character therefore was clearly established by the middle of the 1940s.

However, despite its mass character, the process of political mobilisation of the National Conference was much more addressed to men. There were some women who were visible in the politics of Kashmir in the 1940s and early 1950s, however,

12 It was in 1939 that the National Conference came into existence after the transformation of All Jammu and Kashmir Muslim Conference. The Muslim Conference had been organised in 1932 around the religious identity of Muslims and had not only limited support base but also represented only the emerging middle-class elite of Jammu and Kashmir. Its objectives were also limited to the education and employment of the Muslims of the state. However, the National Conference in comparison was a broad-based organisation with progressive economic and political ideology.

these were elite women and did not represent the mass of ordinary Kashmiri women. Political consciousness though expanding in Kashmir, however, did not mean the equal mobilisation and participation of women.[13]

The reason why there was not much visibility of women in Kashmir's politics was in the general backwardness in Kashmiri society and lack of education among women. While men had started taking to education, and a small class of educated middle class was created among men, there were not many educated women.[14]

13 The major reference to women's mobilisation during the early period of political consciousness in Kashmir is with reference to the social reform movement among the Pandit community. Within this community, there were few educated women who were visible in connection with the social reform campaign. Prem Nath Bazaz has noted the participation of women in the campaign. Referring to the role of the Yuvak Sabha of which he was President, he mentions how this organisation succeeded in mobilising a large number of women. To quote him, 'Public meetings were held in every part of Srinagar which were largely attended. Efforts were made to enlist the cooperation of women in making the scheme a success. In the capacity of the President of Yuvak Sabha, I had to address numerous gatherings in the city, in towns and even in far off villages wherever Pandits live. The lively scenes of enthusiasm are still fresh in my mind. I distinctly remember a meeting which was attended by more than 3000 ladies at Alikadal when a wall had to be demolished to make a big compound adjacent to the meeting grounds available to accommodate the unceasing flow of eager women.' He further notes, 'I also retain in my memory the clear impressions of a huge mile-long funeral procession of men and women which was carried out with a pheran and taranga borne on a plank in the middle, symbolising the death of the discarded attire. It ended at the crematorium on the bank of Dood Ganga. The years 1931-34 were full of zest when Pandit women took a glorious part in the regeneration of the community though in a restricted sphere. Vimla Kaul, Chandadevi, Deviki Koul, Sona Batni (nee Badri) Bazaz and several grown-up girls of the Trust schools were among those who played leading roles in organising the demonstrations (Bazaz, 1959).'

14 Further, the political tradition of Kashmir was quite significantly located within the trade union politics. When there was no other space available for Kashmiris, they would manifest their discontent via the trade union politics. As early as the middle of the nineteenth century, there was a famous strike in the government silk factory. The trade union politics was visible throughout the early twentieth century. However, as the wage labour was mainly the domain of men, the women were not visible in trade union politics as well.

Even so, the politics of the National Conference had expanded the range of political consciousness in Kashmir, and though women were not equally participatory in the street politics as men were, they were still much ahead of women elsewhere in the northern Indian sub-continent. Nearer home, in Jammu region and Ladakh, women were not as politically conscious as women in Kashmir. Jammu region, in fact, lacked the progressive character of politics and unlike Kashmir, it had no political organisation that sought to engage with the marginal classes, including the peasantry, the working classes and the women. Though there was a large population of disgruntled peasantry in this region, mostly Muslims, it had no organisation parallel to the National Conference which could channel their discontent into mass politics. Apart from the oppressed Muslim peasantry, there was a large class of Dalit Hindu landless peasants who were not only economically but also socially oppressed. But the region did not offer any progressive pro-people politics to these socially and economically oppressed people. The National Conference had its major focus on Kashmir and therefore it did not extend itself to Jammu region even in the post-1939 period. The Muslim Conference, the other organisation that had a significant presence in Jammu region, was a religion-oriented and feudal organisation which did not have any agenda for socio-economic emancipation of people.[15] So in this situation, there was no mobilisation of the

15 After merging itself into the National Conference, the Muslim Conference in Jammu region resurrected itself. The Jammu leaders of the Muslim Conference were, from the very beginning, opposed to the idea of changing the character of the Muslim Conference. They opposed the socio-economic ideology of the National Conference and also rejected the idea of opening up this organisation to the non-Muslims.

marginal classes in Jammu region. Hence, the kind of political consciousness that the women of Kashmir could acquire due to the presence of a mass-based political organisation and movement politics was missing in Jammu region.

In Kashmir also, where politics was acquiring intensity, women were generally in the background. While referring to women's presence during a 'martyr's day programme', Krishna Misri thus notes, 'they were the silent background of the animated meeting. And it occurred to me looking at them that they had been the silent background of all the history of Kashmir and the struggles of its people (Cited in Whitehead, 2019,161).'

The Quit Kashmir Movement brought some women into the public space in the Valley. Prem Nath Bazaz, famed and oft-quoted Kashmiri political activist, scholar and author, notes that it was with the Quit Kashmir Movement that the participation of women in public protests started getting registered. He thus states,

> For a whole decade, from 1936-1946, Kashmiri women took little or no part in politics, but were constructively engaged in acquiring literacy and learning. When in May 1946, the National Conference, under the leadership of Sheikh Abdullah, embarked upon 'Quit Kashmir' adventure, politically-minded Muslim women came again to the fore. They actively participated in the demonstrations… Though the participants still came largely from the working classes, a few of them also belonged to upper and educated sections.
>
> (Bazaz, 1959, 262)

It was during this time that the limited presence of women in protest politics was registered. In any case, the ideological blueprint of the National Conference was imagined by a woman – Freda Bedi. Freda Bedi, along with her communist husband, BPL Bedi, had contributed to the writing of the New Kashmir Manifesto (Whitehead, 2019). The husband-wife duo that was earlier actively engaged with the Punjab's Kisan Movement, got involved in Kashmir's politics in 1930s and influenced its ideological framework deeply. Andrew Whitehead, a historian, author and former correspondent and editor of BBC World Service News writes, 'The Bedi's increasing presence in Kashmir coincided with and contributed to – a radical turn in the National Conference. Sheikh Abdullah… relied a great deal on the support and guidance of the Bedis and other communists who visited Kashmir or were based there (Whitehead in an interview with Naseer Ganai, 2019).' Referring to Bedi's role in influencing the politics of Kashmir, Whitehead further notes that 'she certainly played a role in liaising with the underground National Conference leadership after the Maharaja's police had arrested Sheikh Abdullah and many of his colleagues… (Whitehead in an interview with Naseer Ganai, 2019).'

Along with Freda Bedi, who played a very influential role in the politics of National Conference, there was a local woman named Noor Gujri who participated in Kashmir's politics at that time. She was a milkman's daughter who played a leading role in mobilising other women. She was arrested a number of times for her political activities (Bazaz, 1959, 262). Bazaz also refers to Fatima, a peasant woman who was shot dead while leading a procession in 1946. Among other women who emerged as active participants in the movement politics were Akbar Jahan, the wife of Sheikh Abdullah and Zainab Begum. Referring to her role in the Quit Kashmir Movement, Bazaz thus notes,

> After Sheikh Abdullah and his colleagues were arrested in May 1946, the begum broke the shackles that bound her to certain pernicious traditions and customs. She removed the veil, rose equal to the occasion and joined the ranks of freedom fighters. She led the anti-government demonstrations, delivered speeches to maintain the morale of National Conference workers and thus raised the drooping spirit of Abdullah's followers. Collecting donations from charitable sympathisers, she arranged relief for the victims of Dogra aggression.
>
> (Bazaz, 1959, 263)

Zainab Begum was an important member of the National Conference and she participated in the Quit Kashmir Movement. Among other women who became active participants in Kashmir's politics included Mehmooda Ahmed Ali Shah, Sajida Begum and Krishna Misri. All three of them were educationists. Of these, Mehmooda Ahmed Ali Shah identified herself with the left leaning politics of Kashmir.

One oft cited situation when women in Kashmir became visible in the public life occurred in 1947 when women's militia was formed in the wake of the tribal invasion of Kashmir. National Militia was a voluntary force organised for the defence of Kashmir by the National Conference under the leadership of Sheikh Mohammad Abdullah. In the situation in which the Kashmir valley was rendered defenceless, it became the responsibility of the Militia to defend the strategic points in the Valley. Women's Defence Corps was a part of this militia and was comprised only of women. Referring to the formation of Women's militia, Whitehead thus notes,

> The raising of the women's militia was a consequence of the turbulence which followed the end of the British Raj in August 1947 and the independence achieved by India and Pakistan.... The women's section of the militia or the Women's Self Defence Corps as it was known, was established when the threat to Srinagar was still acute. Stories circulated – perhaps exaggerated, but with a basis in fact – that the tribal forces had raped and abducted women, particularly non-Muslims, as they advanced eastwards along the Jhelum river. The idea behind the militia was that the women of Srinagar would be able to defend their honour should the city be overrun.
>
> (Whitehead, 2017)

According to Whitehead, the mobilisation in favour of the militia was done by the communists located in Kashmir.

> It seems only to have mustered in Srinagar and probably to have consisted of under a hundred women, many of them teenagers. The recruits were from all communities, but disproportionately from among the small Kashmiri-speaking Hindu minority, who made up the larger part of professions and liberal intelligentsia in Srinagar.
>
> (Whitehead, 2017)

Though they did not engage in direct war, they were trained in self-defence. As Misri notes,

> They patrolled the city day and night with arms, kept vigil, guarded strategic bridges, approaches to the city, banks, offices, etc. With paramilitary training in weapons, some of them were deployed with army detachments to fight the enemy at war footing.
>
> (Krishna Misri cited in Khan, 2010, 116-117)

Though women who joined this force did not actually enter the battlefield, their role had symbolic value for the Kashmiri society. The participation of women was certainly a result of the familial affiliations to the politics of National Conference. While the young men in the family joined the Militia, the women joined the women's force. As part of the force, the women were given formal military training.[16] Referring to the role that the women's militia played, Krishna Misri thus recounts:

> WSDS [Women's Self-Defense Corps] was in the forefront providing succour to dislocated individuals and families coming from areas ravaged by the barbaric tribesman. It was a formidable challenge. Traumatised, bereft of moorings and uncertain of their future, their dire physical and psychic

---

16 That Women's militia was popular among the educated Kashmiri women gets clear from the memoir of Kanta Wazir who was a college student at the time it was formed and functional, during the 1947-48 period. To quote her, 'I knew about the militia; there was talk about it in every street and lane (gali gali mein baat thi) but I went through my college (SP College). We were told about it by our professors and were encouraged to join if we wanted to (Wazir, 2019).'

> condition required immediate balm. Women leaders alongside volunteers took up the humanitarian work. We visited the camps and helped in the distribution of essential commodities like foodstuff, medicine, warm clothes, etc. Time was spent with the displaced women to provide them emotional support and solace...
>
> (Misri, 2013)

Though it was a short-lived phenomenon, the women's militia became a historic part of Kashmir's politics. 'By the close of 1948, the women's militia had been disbanded and the much larger men's militia was eventually incorporated into India's armed forces (Whitehead, 2017).'

Women and Power Politics

A study of women's presence in power politics clearly shows that women have been quite marginal in this politics. This despite the fact that there has been a great degree of mobilisation of women along with men in the politics of the state, particularly in Kashmir valley. Throughout the post-1947 history of Kashmir's politics, women have been in the forefront in the protest/resistance politics. They are also quite 'political' persons and compared to women of many other places, possess high level of political consciousness. However, their political consciousness and political mobilisation has not helped them to acquire a significant space in the power politics. Their participation in protest politics does not lead either to the assertion of their gender identity or to an increase in their influence within the mainstream politics. There is thus a paradox about women's participation which relates to their near-total absence from positions of power even when they are quite visible in day-to-day politics of protest.

Referring to the paradox of women's visibility in protest politics and their invisibility in power politics, Anuradha Bhasin Jamwal, Executive Editor of *Kashmir Times*, thus notes:

> Women in mainstream politics have been more marginalized with the significance of an agitationist role for women diminishing in the post 1947 scenario. Women have grouped together in struggles and then relegated themselves to the four walls of their homes. But even this tradition does not appear to be universal. While public space for women in a political role is more conspicuous in Kashmir Valley, it is hardly witnessed in Jammu region, barring Poonch, where women were known to have played a role in the pre-partition politics and post-partition communal riots and then gradually slipped into the shadows.
>
> (Jamwal, 2010, 339)

Countering Jamwal, one can argue that women did play a significant role in agitational politics of Jammu in 2008 when they participated in the Amarnath agitation in large numbers. However, one would agree with her, that beyond the agitation, women in Jammu region, as in Kashmir region, failed to take advantage of their political role for their own political empowerment.

A glance at the way the power politics operates in Jammu and Kashmir clearly reflects a huge gap between men and women. Whether as members of political parties, or as contestants, as political leaders or as legislators – their presence at best can be described as a symbolic one. So negligible is their number that they are almost invisible. Beyond voting and attending rallies on behalf of political parties, their political activities within the mainstream politics are minimal. This despite the fact that every political party has a woman's wing, which has a formal structure – with a woman leader and women cadres. However, in reality, the woman's wing remains as a subordinated political organ and has marginal role in the decision making. Rather than rising from the cadre, the women in leadership positions are nominated by the party leaders, and very often they are the relatives of male leaders of the party.

Explaining the absence of women in the public space of Kashmir, Krishna Misri locates the problem in the patriarchal nature of society – in the gender division of roles and dichotomy between the public and private spheres. According to her, even when women were taking up jobs and getting educated, they continued to remain subordinated by the traditional context of gender hierarchy. Referring to the processes of modernisation and entry of women in the public space, she notes the continuity of the traditional patriarchal social norms.

> The Kashmiri women entered the public space, while their domestic conditions continued to be predominated by the outmoded feudal structures and attitudes. Even the social attitudes remained unaltered. Balancing their career choices within these structures added to their responsibilities and burden. While they were coming to grips with their new identities in the public domain, the private domain demanded conventional and traditional roles. The transitional period was tough. There was not much encouragement from the

> families either. Their work and achievements, at times, came to be devalued.
>
> (Misri, 2010, 313)

Misri further notes the pressure that women had to face because of the dual role that they were performing and the lack of personal empowerment.

> They came to be projected as neither good mothers nor good wives, which added to the given 'guilt complex' of a working woman. Majority of working women had little control on their earnings. These contradictions manifested in new forms of social and economic exploitation of women. They could make few choices and assert their subjectivity. The 'limited empowerment' did not enable them to question the unquestioned patriarchal hegemony and power-relations.
>
> (Misri, 2010, 313)

The patriarchal context of society inhibiting women's effective role in decision-making and leadership positions has been underlined by Nyla Ali Khan as well. Nyla Ali Khan, a professor and author of various books, is the granddaughter of Sheikh Abdullah. She finds the patriarchal structure and gender hierarchy responsible for the perpetual subordination of women in various fields of life. She links the structures of patriarchy not only with the absence of women in power politics but also with their subordination in other areas as well. 'Ironically, women in J&K have not yet found niches in the upper echelons of decision-making bodies – political, religious or social.' She refers to 'asymmetrical gender hierarchies' that 'portend the debasement and prostration of women' (Khan, 2010, 123). Such debasement of women, she finds in much of the social, religious or political discourses.

Despite different dimensions of politics, as it takes shape in Jammu and Kashmir, one thing remains common, and that is, when it comes to positions of power, women go missing, even when they may be visible in other spaces. This is as much true of the power politics, as the agitational politics or the conflict politics. In a way, one can say that political decision making in this erstwhile state has been a monopoly of men. As we analyse the role of women in the decision-making positions in each sphere of politics, we will find a similar gender hierarchy. In this chapter, we will focus on the role of women within the formal electoral sphere of politics.

Women in Electoral Politics

As far as electoral politics is concerned, women have failed to become a significant political constituency in Jammu and Kashmir. They are not seen to be voting en bloc as women; they are not seen as a political force significant enough to be wooed by the political parties. This despite the fact that women-related issues form part of the political discourse of various political organisations and parties. However, these issues become mere instruments in their larger political agenda. They are not seen as serious gender issues that need to be dealt with. In Kashmir, for instance, the last three decades of militancy have seen a lot of women-related issues – including those related to human rights, particularly those related to abduction and rape of women, the issue of 'half widows' and many similar issues. These issues were raised not only by the separatists but even by the mainstream leaders. However, rather than raising these issues from the perspective of gender, these leaders were raising them from the perspective of 'political identity'. In fact, gender specificity or gender sensitivity is not to be seen – neither in the electoral manifestoes nor in the electoral campaign. No specific appeal is made to women as voters. No political programmes are specifically targeted at women.

Women as Voters

Women in electoral politics are not visible beyond the level of voting. But initially, even at that level, there was quite a big gap between men and women. The electoral data available for 1972[17] shows that while around 70% men voted during that election, only around 54% women voted. The gap between the male and female voters persisted during the 1977 election, though it was slightly decreased. As against 73% male voters, 60% of the women voters exercised their franchise. However, by 1983, the gap between the male and female voters was quite reduced. As against 75.56% male voters, there were 70.48% female voters. One could see that almost three-fourth of the women voters were exercising their right to vote. This percentage of women voters was maintained through the 1987

17 There is lack of availability of systematic data on electoral politics before the 1972 Assembly election.

election when 70.36% women came out to cast their vote. Though there was a gap of around 8% between male and female voters, yet women had come a long way from 1972 when around half of the women voters did not cast their votes.

The higher female voter participation during the 1977-1987 period can be attributed to very high political mobilisation by the political parties during these elections. The 1977 election was the first such election in Kashmir which developed the reputation of being the most participatory election. The image of the electoral politics in the state, particularly in Kashmir region, was not very positive. There was a general allegation of the electoral politics being manipulated at the official levels. In fact, for a long period, there was no effective electoral exercise as large number of candidates were returned unopposed. Thus, during the first Assembly election held in 1952, all but two seats were returned unopposed. This practice continued till the 1967 Assembly election. During this election also, half of the total seats were returned without any contest. As an implication of this situation, the electoral activity was quite limited and since large number of seats were filled without any process of voting, people did not have much chance to visit the voting booth. This certainly had its implications for the women voters. Unlike the rest of India where women were getting familiarised with the electoral politics and overcoming their inhibitions to come out for the purpose of voting ever since 1951, women of J&K were not getting that opportunity. For them, the process started quite late in the 1970s.

The 1970s was also the period when the democratic process

was getting rooted in Jammu and Kashmir. This was the period when a multi-party competition started taking place. Before that, there was an almost hegemonic control of a single party over the electoral politics – Jammu and Kashmir National Conference (JKNC) from 1951 to 1962 and Congress from 1967 to 1972. The presence of the opposition was quite minimal and whatever limited opposition was visible, it was in Jammu region. But even here, it was quite a weak opposition. The 1977 election was the first such Assembly election where there was a keen competition at the state level among the JKNC, Congress and Janata Party. It was because of this nature of competition that there was a high level of political mobilisation and this was reflected in the voter turnout. The 1983 Assembly election was similarly quite competitive, and with JKNC and Congress involved in an embittered fight, there was quite a high voter turnout. The 1987 Assembly election also was quite competitive with a number of parties contesting the election including the JKNC, Congress, Muslim United Front (MUF) and People's Conference. In Kashmir region, the MUF was a new entrant and quite aggressive in its electoral response. The political environment was charged and therefore there was higher voter participation, of both men and women. The following table reflects the increasing voter participation of women during 1972-1987 period.

Table No 1

Women Voters 1972-1987 Assembly Elections

Year of Election	Percentage of Male Voters	Percentage of Female Voters	Gap between Male and Female Voters
1972	69.27	53.92	15.35
1977	73.14	60.39	12.75
1983	75.56	70.48	5.08
1987	78.65	70.36	8.29

(Source: Election Commission of India)

This table clearly shows how the female voter turnout increased from 53.92% in 1972 to 70.36% in 1987. The relative gap between men and women also decreased over the period.

The political situation in the state, particularly in Kashmir region, changed very drastically after the 1987 Assembly election. Deep political resentment had started setting in after the 1984 overthrow of the JKNC government due to the intervention of the Congress Party. This sense of resentment increased when the JKNC entered into an alliance with the Congress Party in 1986. The general perception that the 1987 Assembly election was manipulated by the two parties (JKNC and the Congress) further aggravated this sense of discontent. While the political resentment in the post-1987 period was reflected in massive protests on the streets of Kashmir in the 1987-1989 period, it was in 1989 that there was onset of armed militancy. One of the major implications of armed militancy and separatism was that democratic politics totally collapsed. For the next seven years, no normal political process could be possible as the level of violence was very high. It was only in 1996 that the next Assembly election could take place. The election process in Kashmir was not normal as militancy was still at its peak. There was no electioneering process in Kashmir region and the candidates could not openly indulge in the electoral campaign. The next election that took place in 2002 was also impacted by militancy. During this election also, normal electioneering could not take place and the voter turnout was quite low. Throughout this period, there was a lot of pressure on the voters in Kashmir region and they could not freely exercise their right to franchise. The militants and separatist organisations would give the call for boycott of elections and there would be a high level of violence during the elections. While the candidates would be targeted, even the voting booths were not safe. This certainly had greater implications for women voters. Though the overall voter turnout was reduced in Kashmir, for women it was quite dismal. Apart from Kashmir region, the voter turnout was also affected in the militancy-infested districts of Jammu region, particularly Poonch, Rajouri and Doda districts. Table 2 presents the data related to male and female voter turnout in the 1996-2014 period. It clearly reflects how voter turnout was impacted by the militancy, and how the gap between male and female voters that was quite decreased by 1987, had increased during the 1996 and 2002 Assembly elections. While female voter turnout was 70.36% in the 1987 Assembly election, it fell to 46.08% in 1996. It was further reduced to 38.27% in the 2002 Assembly election.

It was only with the decline of militancy that the female voter turnout started improving. Though the female voter turnout could not still match with the 1987 turnout, but it was a heartening situation that the gap between the male and female voters was decreasing significantly, and in 2014 more female votes were cast as compared to male votes.

Table No 2

Women Voters 1996-2014 Assembly Elections

Year of Election	Percentage of Male voters	Percentage of Female voters	Gap between Male and Female voters
1996	60.57	46.08	14.49
2002	48.26	38.27	9.99
2008	63.28	58.86	4.42
2014	64.85	66.27	-1.42

(Source: Election Commission of India)

The data of voter turnout during the period of militancy clearly shows how conflict situation impacts women's participation in politics. Already confined to private spaces, conflict situation pushes women further into this space. However, the data also shows that even the male participation was affected by the situation of militancy and like female voter turnout, the male voter turnout was also drastically lowered during this period.

Beyond Voting

Beyond voting, the presence of women in other electoral activities is not comparable to that of men. Lesser number of women identify with party politics and only few join politics and political parties in a formal manner. The Panchayati Raj Institutions that mobilised large number of women in competitive politics elsewhere in India during the last three decades, was very late to come to this state; it is only recently that women have been elected as Panchayat members in large numbers and are joining formal politics as well.

Despite the fact that almost every political party has a woman's wing, the position of women within party politics is quite dismal. Even the Jammu and Kashmir National Conference, which provided a progressive framework of gender equality in the social and political sphere, has not had a very gender-friendly record in its party politics. Despite being the oldest mass party of the state, it could never boast of a large number of women members. Situation has been almost similar for other political parties. Of course, every political party has a woman's wing with women office bearers, women cadres and women members, but these wings are more of a formal arrangement rather than effective channels for women's participation and political growth.

A study of the women's wings of most of the political parties of Jammu and Kashmir shows that their role is mainly confined to organising and coordinating the activities of women members of the party. These wings are also activated for any women-related activities, mostly the election campaigns among women. During these campaigns, the women cadre of the party are expected to address the women-specific rallies. They are also activated for the door-to-door campaign process.

The presence of women's wings is also seen during the protests organised by political parties. This is one area where the women's wings make their presence felt. Women carrying banners and chanting slogans have news value and catch the media attention. Hence, on issues like price rise, law and order issues, water and electricity issues, protests are organised by the political parties with significant presence of women. But when it comes to the structure of the party and its decision-making process, the women's wings do not contribute much. Even for decisions related to women's issues, these wings are not much effective.

On the whole, one can say that within party structures women remain quite marginalised and subordinated. They are generally assigned secondary status and are rarely involved in important decisions of the party. With the exception of few women who rise to decision-making positions within the party, most women remain at the cadre level. Not many women get involved in the organisational structure of the party and hardly any get a chance to contest elections.

Interestingly, the situation does not change even when there is a woman leader at the helm of affairs. A party being headed by a woman or a party where a particular woman may be holding an influential position, does not necessarily ensure a greater number of women in the party's organisational structure or in the decision-making position. This has been true in case of JKNC where Begum Abdullah was quite an influential leader and at one point of time, she was the patron of the party; and even the PDP (Jammu and Kashmir People's Democratic Party) which has been headed by Mehbooba Mufti. Their presence could not be instrumental in bringing more women to the party or placing them in positions of power. Incidentally both these leaders themselves entered politics due to their male relatives – Begum Abdullah being the wife of Sheikh Abdullah and Mehbooba Mufti being the daughter of Mufti Mohammed Sayeed.

That the party politics remains dominated by men has its implications for the electoral politics. Not many women contest elections and even fewer women are able to win elections and hold legislative membership – whether in the Legislative Assembly or in the Parliament. A glance at the electoral data from 1972 to 2014 Assembly elections shows that the percentage of female candidates never exceeded 5% of the total number of candidates. It was the 2008 Assembly election that witnessed the highest percentage (4.95%) of women candidates. Earlier, in the 2002 Assembly election, the percentage of women candidates was close to the percentage in 2008. 4.23% of the candidates in this election were women. Otherwise, the percentage of women candidates has been still more dismal. This percentage was as low as 0.97% in 1977, 1.38% in 1983, 1.46% in 1996, 2.33% in 1972 and 2.46% in the 1987 Assembly election. One can see that the percentage of women candidates was slightly increased during the 2002 and 2008 elections, however, in 2014, the percentage of female candidates fell to 3%.

Table No 3

Women Candidates 1972-2014 Assembly Elections

Year of Election	Total Number of Candidates	Number of Female Candidates	Percentage of Female Candidates
1972	342	8	2.33
1977	409	4	0.97
1983	505	7	1.38
1987	528	13	2.46
1996	1027	15	1.46
2002	709	30	4.23
2008	1354	67	4.94
2014	831	28	3.0

(Source: Election Commission of India)

Following is a detailed analysis of women candidates during various Assembly elections.

During the 1972 Assembly election, only 8 of the 342 candidates were women. While four of these candidates represented the Indian National Congress, which was the ruling party at that time, the remaining were independents.[18] The number of women contestants was smallest in 1977 when only four women joined the election fray. The percentage of women candidates in this election was less than one percent. Three of these candidates belonged to the ruling party at the Centre, the Janata Party, and one was an independent candidate.[19]

18 Among the Congress candidates included Zainab Begum (Amira Kadal, Kashmir Division), Hajra Begum (Banihal, Kashmir division), Nirmal Devi (Tikri, Jammu division) and Shanta Bharti (Jandrah Gharota, Jammu Division).

19 The candidates for Janata Party included Jagmohini (Habbakadal, Kashmir Division), Gurbachan Kumari (Bari Brahmana, Jammu Division), and Parkash Rani (Basohli, Jammu division). Shanta Bharti, meanwhile was an independent candidate (Jammu East).

The number of women candidates was slightly increased in the subsequent elections, however, their percentage remained quite minimal. There were seven women candidates during the 1983 elections (1.38%) and thirteen during the 1987 Assembly elections (2.46%). While there was one candidate each from BJP and National Conference, five were independent candidates.[20] All these candidates belonged to Jammu division. There were no women candidates either from Kashmir or Ladakh.

Of the thirteen women candidates during the 1987 Assembly election, nine were independent candidates.[21] Three woman candidates were fielded by Panthers Party and one was fielded by INC.[22] This time also there was no female candidate either from Kashmir or Ladakh regions. All the female candidates were fielded in Jammu region.

In 1996, when the number of candidates was increased twofold compared to the 1983 and 1987 elections, the number of female candidates remained quite low. Of the 1027 candidates, only 15 were women. This made for less than two percent of the total candidates. The low number of women candidates during this election can be related to the militancy which was at its peak during this election. Due to

---

20 While the BJP candidate was Prakash Rani (Basohli), the NC candidate was Gurbachan Kumari (Bari Brahmana). Five independent candidates included Vimla Sharma (R.S. Pura), Jaya Mala (Jammu Cantonment), Sandal Devi (Marh), Jaswanti (Nowshera).

21 These included Gurbachan Kumari (Bari Brahmana), Suman Dogra (Bishnah), Pushp Lata (Jammu West), Shanti Devi (Jammu East), Ram Piyari Khajuria (Jammu East), Vidya Devi (Jammu East), Jaswanti Devi (Nowshera), Saire Begam (Rajouri).

22 The Panthers Party candidates included, Sudarshan Sambyal (Samba), Jai Mala (Jammu East), and Sunita Devi (Chhamb). Swaran Lata (Bari Brahmana)] was INC candidate.

the overall environment of violence, women had withdrawn from the public space and that is the reason the percentage of the female voters was also very low. Of the fifteen candidates, five were fielded by the Congress Party, two candidates were fielded by BJP and one candidate each was fielded by JKNC, JD and Panthers Party. There were three independent women candidates.[23]

The number of women candidates was increased to thirty in 2002 and this was by far the largest number and percentage of women contestants. As against the 1.46% female contestants in 1996, it was 4.23% of the total candidates in 2002. Of these, four women were fielded by the Congress Party, four candidates were fielded by the National Conference, and four female candidates were fielded by the PDP also; two candidates each were fielded by SJP (R) and Panthers Party; and one

23 The Congress candidates included Mehbooba Mufti (Bijbehara, Kashmir); Gulshan Akhtar (Pahalgam, Kashmir); Amrit Barsha (Ramban, Jammu); Swaran Lata (Samba); Rani Gargi Blowria (Vijaypur). The BJP candidates were Sarla Taploo (Habbakadal) and Spalzes Angmo (Leh, Ladakh). JKNC candidates was Sakina Akhtar (Noorabad, Kashmir), JD candidates were Mehbooba (Batamaloo, Kashmir) and Gurbachan Kumari Rana (Vijaypur, Jammu), and Panthers Party candidate was Taja Begum (Handwara, Kashmir). The Independent candidates were Hafiza Begum (Sonawar, Kashmir), Amrita Bhat (Doda, Jammu), Kanta Devi Sharma (Gandhi Nagar, Jammu).

candidate each by JDS, LJNSP and JD (U). The rest of the candidates were Independent.[24]

The number of women candidates increased to sixty-seven in the 2008 election. The total number of candidates was 1354. The percentage of female candidates had increased to 4.94%. Of these, the highest number of women (twenty-one) was of Independent candidates.[25] From political parties, there were nine female contestants from PDP; seven from JKNPP; five from BJP; four from Congress; four from BSP; three from JKANC; two each from NC , LJP and BCP and one each from

---

24 The Congress candidates included Suman Lata Bhagat (R.S. Pura, Jammu), Swarn Lata (Samba), Amreen Badar (Budgam, Kashmir), Khem Lata Wakhloo (Sonawar, Kashmir,); the JKNC candidates included Shameema (Habba Kadal, Kashmir), Nishat Akhtar (Wachi, Kashmir), Sakeena Akhtar (Noorabad, Kashmir), Bimla Luthra (Jammu East); PDP candidates included Shanti Devi (Nagrota, Jammu), Kriti Verma (Kathua), Mumtaz Kouser (Gulabgarh, Jammu), Mehbooba Mufti (Pahalgam, Kashmir); SJP (R) candidates included Minu Jamwal, (Gandhi Nagar, Jammu) and Vijay Rajya Pathania, (Billawar, Jammu); Panthers Party candidates included Sudesh Puri, (Bishnah, Jammu) and Shameema Begum, (Batamaloo, Kashmir). Balvinder Kour was from JDS, Tripta Kumari Vaid was fielded by LJNSP, Afroza Tabasum by JD (U) (Amira Kadal, Kashmir). The Independent candidates included Vijay Chib (Suchetgarh, Jammu), Rita Jitendera (Jammu East, Jammu), Noor Jahan (Jammu East, Jammu), Santosh Suri (Reasi, Jammu), Kamla Devi (Ramban, Jammu), Hafeeza Begum (Pampore, Kashmir), Khalida Tabasum (Amira Kadal, Kashmir), Hafiza Begum (Sonawar, Kashmir).

25 These included Shabnam Gani Lone, Gousia Bashir, Shakeela Bano, Irshada Akhtar, Rabia, Jabeena Jan, Khazana Azeez, Sabiya Qadiri, Afroza Qadir, Aisha Parveen, Rashida Akbar, Jawahira Begum, Meenakshi Sharma, Pushpa Devi, Geeta Thakur, Anju Koul, Kanchan Sharma, Gurbachan Kumari Rana, Raj Mohani Sharma, Neelam Devi, Mohinder Kour).

NCP, SAP, AIF, JSM, RK, SDP, JKPDF. [26]

The number of female contestants was quite reduced during the 2014 Assembly elections. As against sixty-seven candidates in the 2008 election, there were only twenty-eight candidates in these elections and from 4.94% women candidates, their percentage was reduced to 3%. Of these, seven were independent candidates; six from JKNC; three each from Congress, BJP and SP; two from JKNPP; and one each from PDP, RPI, BHBP and BSP .[27]

On the whole, there clearly seems to be a reluctance among political parties to field female candidates, mostly because of less number of women in positions where they can be given party tickets.

26 The PDP candidates included Asiea, Asifa Tariq Qara, Mehbooba Mufti, Sahar Iqbal, Mumtaz Kouser, Shamshad Bano, Anita Devi, Surjeet Kour, Shanti Devi. The JKNPP candidates included Shafiqa Begum, Raja Begum, Shameema Begum, Parveen Akhtar Bhat, Rafiqa Akhtar, Anita Kumari, Tabbasum Bano. The BJP candidates included Halima Bano, Sheila Bhat, Sweeti Koul, Satwant Kour, Shilpi Verm. The Congress candidates included Ahmreen Badar, Khem Lata Wakhloo, Kanta Andotra, Suman Lata Bhagat. BSP candidates included Saiyda Bagum, Hanifa Bagum, Rano Devi, Sheraz Begum Mirza. JKANC candidates included Rafiqa Bano, Aisha Nishat, Neelam Devi; JKNC candidates included Shameema Firdous, Sakina Ittoo; LJP candidates included Mumtaz Begum Salaria, Sudesh Puri; BCP candidates included Nusrat Bano, Sarita Sharma. Rest of them were NCP (Saira Sameer), SAP (Gulshana Parveen), AIFB (Hajira), SP (Amrit Barsha), JSM(P) (Swarn Sharma), RKSP (Veena Dogra), SDP (Saleema Begum), JKPDF (Parveen).

27 NC candidates included Shamima Firdous, Sakina Ittoo, Shamshad Bano, Satwant Kaur, Bimla Luthra, Shakti Bala. Congress candidates included Shameema Raina, Khem Lata Wakhloo, Suman Lata Bhagat. The BJP candidates included Neelam Gaash, Heena Shafi Bhat, Darakshan Andrabi. The SP candidates included Amrit Barsha, Pushpa Devi, Bimla Devi Mottan. JKNPP candidates included Anita Kumari and Kosar Parveen. Female candidates from other parities included PDP (Asiea), RPI (Suriaya Bano), BHBP (Kanchan Sharma) and BSP (Sheraz Begum). The seven independent candidates included Haneefa Begum, Mehbooba Shadab, Rashida Mir, Nuzhat Iqbal Zargar, Rano Devi, Meenakshi Sharma, Madhu Bala.

Table No 4

Party Affiliation of Female Candidates
1972-2014 Assembly Elections

Year of Election	Total Number of Female Candidates	INC	NC	BJP	Panthers	Janata	PDP	JD
1972	08	04	-	-	-	-	-	-
1977	04	-	-	-	-	03	-	-
1983	07	-	01	01	-	-	-	-
1987	13	01	-	-	03	-	-	-
1996	15	05	01	03	01	-	-	02
2002	30	04	04	-	02	-	04	-
2008	67	04	02	05	07	-	09	-
2014	28	03	06	03	02	-	01	-

(Source: Election Commission of India)

As most of the active women party members are positioned at the lower levels and are not encouraged to rise up in their political career within the party, they do not get tickets to contest elections. That is the scene of women in almost every political party. It is the reason why a large number of women who contest elections do it as independent candidates rather than as party candidates.

Not only candidature, the success rate of women in Legislative Assembly elections is equally dismal. Year after year, very few women make it up to the decision-making forum of the state. In 1972, four women got elected to the Assembly which is by far the largest number elected in the erstwhile state. In comparison, only one woman got elected in the 1977 and 1987 elections, while no woman got elected in the 1983 elections. In 1996 and 2002, two women candidates got elected. The number of woman legislators rose to three in 2008 and again settled at two in the 2014 elections. In terms of percentages, women did not even form 5% of the total seats of the Legislative Assembly. But even that percentage was achieved only in 1972, after which, the percentage of women legislators was much lower. While women formed only 3.45% of the total legislators in 2008, their percentage was less than 3 in the 1996, 2002 and 2014 legislative Assembly, and less than 2 in 1977 and 1987 respectively. The female winners formed such a miniscule percentage of the total seats of the Legislative Assembly that it is doubtful they could have contributed to the policy making in the erstwhile state.

Table No 5
Women Winners
1972-2014 Assembly Elections

Year of Election	Total number of Seats	Total number of Female Winners	Percentage of Female Winners to Total Seats
1972	75	04	5.33
1977	75	01	1.33
1983	76	Nil	Nil
1987	76	01	1.32
1996	87	02	2.29
2002	87	02	2.29
2008	87	03	3.45
2014	87	02	2.29

(Source: Election Commission of India)

The winnability of women candidates i.e. the percentage of female winners to total female candidates presents a mixed picture. In 1972, percentage of female winners to total female candidates was 50% as four out of eight female candidates won which depicted high winnability. But, in the subsequent elections, their winnability was quite reduced; while it was 25% in 1977, in later elections, it was as low as 13.33% in 1996, 7.69% in 1987, 7.14% in 2014, 6.66% in 2002 and 4.47% in 2008.

Table No 6

Percentage of Women Contestants Compared to Percentage of Women Winners 1972-2014 Assembly Elections

Election	Total Candidates	Female Candidates	Percentage of Female Candidates	Total Number of Female Winners	Percentage of Female Winners to Total female Candidates
1972	342	8	2.33	4	50%
1977	409	4	0.97	1	25%
1983	505	7	1.38	-	-
1987	528	13	2.46	1	7.69
1996	1027	15	1.46	2	13.33
2002	709	30	4.23	2	6.66
2008	1354	67	4.94	3	4.47
2014	831	28	3.0	2	7.14

What has been the party affiliation of women candidates? And how do they perform compared to the independent candidates? As the data shows, though all parties are reluctant in fielding women candidates, yet women with party affiliations have greater chances of winning the election. In 1972, all the female candidates who won the elections belonged to the Congress Party, while all those who lost were independent candidates. In 1977, all female candidates, barring one, belonged to the Janata Party. Only one woman contested the election as an independent candidate. The only winning woman candidate belonged to the Janata Party. In 1983, while independent candidates outnumbered the party candidates, none of them could win the election. In 1987, there were nine independent candidates and none could make it. The only winning candidate belonged to the Congress Party. In 1996, as party candidature to women increased, the number of independent candidates was reduced to three. Of the two winning candidates, one belonged to National Conference and one to the Janata Dal. In 2002 elections, eight independent candidates formed the largest chunk of woman candidates, but of the two winning candidates, one belonged to PDP and the other to Congress. The 2008 Assembly election saw a large number of independent women candidates – a total of twenty-one, but none of them could win the election. Of the three women candidates who were elected, two belonged to JKNC and one to PDP. In 2014, there were seven independent candidates. Of the two women who were elected, one belonged to JKNC and the other to PDP.

Without the active support of the parties, without exposure and training, women fail to perform in the electoral arena. A large number of women who contest elections end up forfeiting their deposits. In 1972, out of eight candidates, half had to forfeit their deposits. In 1983, all of the contestants, but one, forfeited their deposits. Likewise, in 1987, eleven of the thirteen lost their deposits. Though in 1996, things improved slightly as ten out of fifteen candidates could save their deposits, but the situation reversed in 2002 as twenty-six out of thirty woman contestants had to forfeit the deposits. The situation did not improve as fifty-six out of sixty-seven and twenty-five out of twenty-eight female candidates lost their deposits in the years 2008 and 2014 respectively.

Table No 7

Percentage of Women Contestants Forfeiting Deposits 1972-2014 Assembly Elections

Year of Election	Total Number of Female Contestants	Number of Female Candidates who Forfeited Deposits
1972	08	04
1977	-	-
1983	07	06
1987	13	11
1996	15	05
2002	30	26
2008	67	56
2014	28	25

(Source: Election Commission of India)

There are certain peculiarities related to women contestants that need to be highlighted. First, the reserved constituencies (SC) reflect better participation of women as contestants compared to the general seats. For instance, the only woman who won in the 1977 elections belonged to a reserved constituency. Likewise, every subsequent election saw the fielding of women from reserved constituencies. In 1983, 1987 and 1996 elections, two out of seven, five out of thirteen and two out of fifteen women contested elections from reserved constituencies respectively. Likewise, in 2002, there were three woman candidates from reserved constituencies. Six women contested from reserved constituencies, both in the 2008 and 2014 Assembly elections. In terms of percentages, of all the women contestants, women from reserved constituencies formed 38.56% in the 1987 Assembly election, 28.57% in 1983, 25% in 1977, and 21.42% in the 2014 Assembly election.

Table No 8
Female Candidates from Reserved Constituencies
1972-2014 Assembly Elections

Year of Election	Total Number of Female Candidates	Total Number of Candidates from reserved Constituencies	Percentage of Candidates from Reserved Constituencies to Total Female Candidates
1972	08	-	-
1977	04	01	25%
1983	07	02	28.57%
1987	13	05	38.56%
1996	15	02	13.33%
2002	30	03	10%
2008	67	06	8.95%
2014	28	06	21.42%

Another peculiarity relates to the regional differences. Of all the three regions of the erstwhile state of Jammu and

Kashmir, it is from Jammu region that women have been more forthcoming as contestants. The Ladakh region fares the worst in this context. With the exception of 1996 Assembly election when one woman contested, women have remained mostly out of the contest in other elections. While all the female candidates in 1983 and 1987 Assembly elections (seven and thirteen respectively) were fielded from Jammu, in all other Assembly elections, except 2008, the number of female candidates was certainly larger in this region. In 2008, Kashmir region took the lead as thirty-six of the sixty-seven female candidates were fielded here compared to thirty-one of Jammu region. One can see that since 1996, the number of female candidates is increasing.

Table No 9

Women Contestants: Regional Difference
1972-2014 Assembly Elections

Year of Election	Total Female Contestants	Female Contestants from Kashmir	Female Contestants from Jammu	Female Contestants from Ladakh
1972	08	03	05	Nil
1977	04	01	03	Nil
1983	07	Nil	07	Nil
1987	13	Nil	13	Nil
1996	15	07	07	01
2002	30	14	16	Nil
2008	67	36	31	Nil
2014	28	12	16	Nil

Till very recently, the State Assembly, as per the Constitution of the state, reserved two seats in the Assembly for women members. These women were to be nominated by the government and were over and above the fixed number of legislators of the state. However, rather than empowering women, this provision became a tool in the hands of the government to reward the party loyalists who could not make their entry in politics by contesting elections. In some cases, when the male loyalists could not make it, then their wives or any other relative would be obliged through this route.

On the whole, there has been rather an invisibility of women in the state's legislature and executive. The dismal number of elected female representatives has had its implications on their position as Ministers. As elsewhere, very few women could make it to the cabinet, and even when they entered this exclusive male-dominated space, they were generally given 'women-friendly' portfolios. Usually, they would be adjusted in the portfolios related to Social Welfare, Women and Child Development, and so on. With the exception of Mehbooba Mufti who rose to be a leader in her own right and could become the Chief Minister of the state, there were not many instances of women holding important portfolios and making space for themselves as powerful ministers.

Parliamentary Elections and Women

While there have been seventeen Lok Sabha elections in the country, there are only six instances of J&K women's entry into this august House. Krishna Mehta was the first woman to be a Member of Parliament from this state. However, rather than being elected, she was nominated as a member of the Rajya

Sabha in 1957. (Till 1962, all J&K seats to Rajya Sabha and even Lok Sabha were filled through the process of nomination. It was only in 1967 that the jurisdiction of the Election Commission of India was extended to the state; and in 1967 and thereafter, the Members of Parliament were duly elected).

It was only in the year 1977 that two women from J&K could be elected to the Lok Sabha. Of these, one was from Ladakh (Rani Parvati Devi, Queen Mother of Ladakh) and the other was from Kashmir (Begum Akbar Jehan Abdullah). Begum Akbar Jehan repeated her success in the year 1984 for the eighth Lok Sabha. Thereafter, in the year 2004, after a gap of twenty years, Mehbooba Mufti won the Parliamentary elections to enter the Lok Sabha. She again won the Lok Sabha seat in 2014. It is pertinent to note that all the women who could reach the Parliament were either part of the elite families or belonged to the political families of the state.

Women as Decision Makers: A Note on Women Leaders

One gets a fair idea about the role of women in the political decision making if we analyse the role of women leaders in Jammu and Kashmir. Following is a case analysis of various women leaders of J&K who played some role in formal electoral politics.

Of all the visible faces of women in formal politics, the face of Begum Abdullah has been the most prominent one. Though she was thrown in politics as the spouse of Sheikh Abdullah, she carved a political space for herself as a Member of Parliament and as patron of the National Conference. She came from quite an elite background as the daughter of the British hotelier, Michael Harry Nedou (elder son of a European owner of a chain of Indian hotels). Being an educated woman, she became well-exposed to the politics of Kashmir right from the start of her married life. Later, as her husband remained incarcerated for a long period, she played the major role of 'filling in' for her husband. The first time that she took the place of her husband was during the Quit Kashmir Movement when Sheikh Abdullah was jailed. But as Malik[28] notes, rather than decision making, her role at that time was focused more on social activities like raising money and collecting donations. Malik observes that her entry into politics was 'based on her gendered role as wife of the first prime minster of Kashmir and subsequently mother of Farooq Abdullah' (Malik, 2019, 33). She continued to play that role after the long incarceration of Sheikh in the post-1953 period (Khan, 2014). It was gendered identity in politics that despite being a Member of Parliament a number of times and patron of National Conference for a long time, she was known as *Madar-e-Meharban* (Kind Mother).

However, despite the gendered nature of her role in Kashmir's politics, Akbar Jehan proved her mettle as a parliamentarian after the 1977 parliamentary election. She could repeat her winning streak in 1984 even in the midst of party turmoil. This was soon after Farooq Abdullah's government was ousted

28 Inshah Malik is a Gender Studies scholar who has worked extensively on gender issues in Kashmir.

by the intervention of the Central Government. As committed to the ideology of National Conference, she served the party long after her husband's death and remained a force to be reckoned with. For a long time, she was the patron of this party (Khan, 2014). In a world of male-dominated politics with few women role models to emulate, her very presence in Kashmir's politics was quite significant. As Malik notes, 'Akbar Jehan's heroic role opened the way for other women to enter the public political sphere.' With her presence, a space was created for other women, especially from upper classes, to be visible in politics (Malik, 2019, 40).

Among the women who were visible in politics and were relatively prominent in the early post-Accession period was Zainab Begum. She came from a political family as her brother Ghulam Mohammed Sadiq was a prominent leader of Kashmir and later became the Chief Minister of the State. She contested the Assembly election in 1972 and won. As sister of the Chief Minister, she had significant influence in Kashmir's politics.

A woman who did not come from a political family but evolved along with Kashmir's politics was Mehmooda Ahmed Ali Shah. She joined politics as a young student and played a role in the Women's Militia organised by the National Conference to mobilise people for self-defence in the wake of the tribal invasion in 1947. Along with her sister Sajida, she played a major role in mobilising women at that time. To quote Whitehead, she was known to be a left-wing activist and 'was the leading woman on [in] the communist-aligned wing of the National Conference. She was a key figure in the formation and recruitment of the Women's Self Defence Corps (Whitehead, 2007).' Later she emerged as the most significant educationist heading the premium women's college of Srinagar. She was known to be a pioneer in the field of women's education. She was an influential person in her own right – not only in the field of women's education but also in politics. Though she was not formally a part of politics, she had a political aura due to her friendship with Indira Gandhi and GM Sadiq (Inshah Malik, 2019, 33). It was after her retirement that she joined All India Congress Committee as a general secretary and remained a member of the Congress till her death.

More recently, there have been a few women politicians who occupied a significant place in competitive politics. These include Sakina Ittoo and Mehbooba Mufti. What is common for both these women politicians is that both came into politics via the family channel. Sakina Ittoo is the daughter of a senior National Conference leader who was assassinated by militants. It was after the killing of her father during the 1996 Assembly elections that she was pushed into politics abruptly, without being given a choice. At that time, she was training to be a doctor and was in the final year of her medical course. She was the choice of the party for filling up the 'family vacancy' and contesting the election from her father's constituency, Noorabad. Since 1996, she has been consistently contesting elections from the same constituency as a JKNC candidate. She is one of those few women members of the JKNC who not only won the elections a number of times but has also held ministerial posts – in 1996 under Farooq Abdullah's Ministry and in 2008 under Omar Abdullah's Ministry. Since her entry into politics, she has faced tough times. After her father's assassination, she has been a consistent target for the militants. During every election, she has faced serious militant attacks. During the 2002 elections, she faced multiple militant attacks.

Mehbooba Mufti, like Sakina Ittoo, joined politics through her father's patronage. However, once she joined politics, she was able to carve a significant political space for herself. Despite the dynastic route of her entry into politics, one can count Mehbooba Mufti as a significant political leader of Kashmir in her own right. As the leader and the co-architect of the People's Democratic Party, she played an important role in the politics of Kashmir. Soon after the launch of the party in 1999, she was involved in the process of political mobilisation. As part of the 'Healing Touch' policy of the PDP, she moved from village to village of Kashmir to develop personal contact with people and offered them succour in the context of the conflict situation. She, in fact, became a face of the new politics within the mainstream sphere. It was because of her significant presence that the PDP could popularise itself and could win sufficient number of seats during the 2002 Assembly elections and be part of the coalition government along with the Congress and other parties. Though she did not join the government at that time, she was known as the most influential leader of the party, besides her father. Along with the Assembly elections, she contested the Parliamentary elections a number of times and represented South Kashmir in Parliament. She eventually became the first woman Chief Minister of the erstwhile State of

Jammu and Kashmir after the death of her father.

As the Woman President of PDP, the role of Mehbooba Mufti vis-à-vis women's question in J&K has been full of paradoxes. Though she is represented as the first woman leader of Kashmir who played quite an effective role in Kashmir's politics, she did not always take a gender-sensitive position. One of the situations in which she actually took a negative stand on a women-related question revolved around the discrimination against women in the State Subject Law of the state, about which reference has been made above. After the High Court of J&K set aside the discriminatory nature of this law, as the President of the ruling PDP, she pushed a bill in the state legislature which sought to undo the relief provided by the High Court. Known as the Women Disqualification Bill, it sought to disqualify women marrying outside the state from their right to be considered as Permanent Residents of the state.

However, after becoming the Chief Minister, she sought to pursue a few gender-friendly policies within the state. Some of these policies were related to providing special women's buses, abolishing stamp duties for women registering their property and establishing all-women police stations. However, other than that, not much attention was paid by her government to empower women. Though she was able to mobilise women for ground level work, not many women could attain prominent positions within the PDP at any point of time.

Along with Sakina Ittoo and Mehbooba Mufti, one can also refer to Shabnam Lone who joined politics through the dynastic route. Shabnam Lone is the daughter of separatist

Abdul Gani Lone. Lone was initially a prominent mainstream political leader who had formed People's Conference but joined separatist politics in 1989. He was assassinated in a militant attack in 2001. It was after his assassination that claims to the legacy of Lone were made initially by two male children of Lone and quite later by his daughter Shabnam Lone. Since the People's Conference continued to have a political space even after his assassination, Lone's two sons, Bilal Lone and Sajad Lone, were the earlier claimants. Bilal Lone who continued to remain in the separatist politics could not make much use of this legacy, but Sajad Lone who shifted to mainstream politics in 2004 was quite successful in leading the People's Conference. Shabnam Lone, a practitioner of the legal profession, later joined the electoral space and contested the Assembly election. Though Shabnam failed to win the election, her case of entry into politics is interesting from the perspective of challenging the male monopoly in claiming the family's political legacy. Though she contested as an independent candidate in the 2008 Assembly election, her contest from Handwara was with the expectation of getting political gain from her father's political legacy in that constituency. At the time when she took the decision to contest the election, both her brothers were actively involved in the 'boycott politics' – mobilising people not to vote for elections as per the separatist agenda. Her participation therefore was a challenge not only to the family, particularly her two brothers' political position, but also to the separatist politics. By contesting elections at a time when the separatists had given a call for boycott, and when her family including her prominent brothers were supporting the boycott, she had declared an autonomy for her own politics. While campaigning, Shabnam was making use of the popular sentiments for her father's politics. Referring to her decision to contest the election, she thus stated, 'It's a decision guided by the sentiments of my father's supporters (Ramesh Vinayak, 2008).'

One can also include Khalida Shah, a leader of the Awami National Conference, in the list of women who joined politics through the dynastic route. As the eldest daughter of Sheikh Abdullah, and wife of GM Shah – the rival of Farooq Abdullah – who formed Awami National Conference, she became part of the politics because of her husband's political role in Kashmir. After his death, she became the president of the party. She also contested the 2008 Assembly election.

Among other women political leaders of Kashmir, there are a few who have attained some visibility. They include Darakhshan Andrabi, Hina Bhat, Asiea Naqash and Safina Baig. Many of them are there due to their familial connections; for instance, Hina Bhat of BJP is the daughter of JKNC leader Mohammad Shafi Bhat, Asiea Naqash of PDP is the sister-in-law of Tariq Hameed Karra and Safina Baig is the wife of Muzaffar Hussain Baig.

What is the situation of women leaders in Jammu and Ladakh regions? Except for one woman who contested the parliamentary election, there have not been many women coming forward in Ladakh to contest elections and to hold political offices. She was Rani Parvati Devi Deskit Wangmo. Belonging to the Royal family of Ladakh, she was little known outside Ladakh, but held a distinct place in the Ladakh region in her own right. Though she received only primary education, she got to display her agency very early in life. Her husband, the titular king of Ladakh, died young, leaving her behind with four children. She put up a brave front while fighting local traditions to resist her marriage with her brother-in-law, and in fact, ousted him from the palace (She later devised some compensatory mechanism for him). Rani Parvati Devi is Founder-President of Namgyal Institute of Research on Ladakh Art and Culture (NIRLAC) and she did a lot of work in the social field in Ladakh. In 1977, she was made a candidate for Lok Sabha elections by the Indian National Congress (INC) from Ladakh Constituency. Since, J&K National Conference was in coalition with INC in those elections, she won the elections and became the first woman MP from Ladakh.

In Jammu region, the number of women who contest elections has been larger than that of Kashmir, however, one can name only a few women who have reached positions of power or have emerged as political leaders in their own right.

Belonging to the Kishtwar district of Jammu region, Krishna Mehta (1913-93) was the first woman Member of Parliament from the erstwhile state of J&K. Though she was nominated to the post, she has much to her credit in terms of work and spirit of politics in the State. Krishna Mehta was not only born into an eminent family, but was also married into one; her husband (Duni Chand Mehta) was Wazir-e-Wazarat of Muzaffarabad (now in Pakistan). During the tribal invasion, her husband died and she ended up in a refugee camp in Delhi with her young children. Thereafter, she worked tirelessly amongst refugees and suffering women as well as children to attract the attention of Pandit Jawaharlal Nehru and earned herself the nomination to the second Lok Sabha in 1957 from the State of Jammu and Kashmir. Her contribution in bringing Gandhi Seva Sadan and the Khadi Gram Udyog Sangh to the state of J&K was immense. Thus, Krishna Mehta was one woman from the Jammu region whose role in the field of social work and in addressing the sufferings of people, especially women and children of Jammu region, was enormous.

Shanta Bharati was another leader who contested elections a number of times and was a well-known name in the region. She contested the Assembly election from Samba constituency in Jammu region in 1962 as an independent candidate. Although she lost her deposit, it acted as a foundation for her future role in politics. She didn't contest the next elections in 1967 but continued working in the social field. In 1972, the Indian National Congress gave her a ticket for contesting in the Assembly elections from the Jandrah Gharota constituency and she won comfortably. In the very next elections, in the year 1977, she again contested as an independent candidate from Jammu East Constituency. She again lost both the seat and the deposit. Her case clearly reflects that she had the capacity to win the election if a party fielded her as a candidate. Contesting elections as an independent candidate made her winning chances so poor that every time she contested as an independent candidate, she lost her deposit. However, Shanta Bharati was an active woman politician of the region who dared to enter the so-called male bastion of politics. There have been few other women who have been contesting elections and holding some role in party politics.

Women in Grassroots Politics

Panchayati Raj Institutions (PRIs) not only act as major drivers of grassroots empowerment, but are also instrumental in bringing politics and political training grounds to women in the rural areas. J&K has had the provision for establishing panchayats since 1935 when the Village Panchayat Regulation Act No 1 was promulgated by the Dogra rule in the state. Comprising of elected and nominated members and having only judicial powers, those panchayats hardly fulfilled the purpose of local self-governance. Though amendment in the act in 1941 under Dogra rule promised to empower the panchayats, but such an empowerment could not take place.

In the post-Accession period, the mantle fell on the National Conference to strengthen grassroots democracy. This party had made commitment for democratic decentralisation in its ideological blueprint, the Naya Kashmir Manifesto, adopted by the party in 1944. In 1951, the existing Panchayat Raj Act was amended, and following the Balwant Rai Mehta Committee's recommendations, the Village Panchayat Act was introduced in 1958. However, noting much could be achieved at the ground level.

The promulgation of the Jammu and Kashmir Panchayati Raj Act, 1989 was considered a watershed moment in the history of Panchayati Raj Institutions in the erstwhile state of

J&K. It was believed that the Act would introduce some radical changes in the direction of empowering the rural bodies of self-governance. It sought to establish the three-tier system of Panchayati Raj at Halqa, Block and District levels in the state. The Act not only reduced the age of voting from twenty-one to eighteen but also mandated the elections to the panchayats in case of their suspension. It also empowered the panchayats to prepare as well as implement the plans and programs in the fields of education, health, employment, etcetera in rural areas. But, the onset of armed militancy in the state coincided with the arrival of the Act and hence the rules related to the Act could not be made. The elections under the aforesaid Act could take place only in the year 2001. Elections, under this Act have actually taken place only thrice – in 2001, 2011 and latest in 2018.

The 73rd Amendment to the Constitution of India took place in the year 1993. Through this amendment, the Panchayati Raj Institutions acquired a uniform three-tier structure for the whole country along with the constitutional status for them. But, the jurisdiction of the Act could not be extended to the erstwhile state of J&K due to the special status of the state under Article 370 of the Constitution. As a result, the State Act remained inadequate and could not contribute in the process of democratic decentralisation. There were lots of flaws in the Act related to devolution of powers and responsibilities and reservation for SCs, STs, and women. There was also no provision for the State Election Commission and the State Finance Commission.

While the 73rd Amendment Act provided for reservation of seats for the Scheduled Castes and Scheduled Tribes in proportion to their population and to women to the extent of 33% seats through direct election, the 1989 Act outlined that, 'If the prescribed authority is of the opinion that women are not adequately represented in the Halqa Panchayat, it may nominate such number of women to be members thereof, as it may deem fit, provided that the number does not exceed 33% of the total number of the Panchs.' The government could also nominate the Scheduled Caste and Scheduled Tribe members to the Panchayats. So, the representation of women, SCs and STs which was made a constitutional right by the 73rd Amendment, in the case of this state, was at the mercy of the state government.

These flaws were dealt with later. In 2004, provision was made for reservation of seats for SCs, STs and women at the first tier of Panchayats. By later amendments, the provision for State Election Commission as well as State Finance Commission was also made.

The Panchayat election under the 1989 Act took place in 2001. But since there was no provision for women's reservation, very few women could make it up to the position of *panch*. Of the total 20,558 panch constituencies (10,468 in Kashmir and 10,090 in Jammu), only 237 positions (71 in Kashmir division and 166 in Jammu) went to women. Women panch members thus constituted only 1.7% of the total number. The situation was still worse in the case of *sarpanch*. Only 9 out of the total 2700 sarpanchs were women. Of these nine women sarpanchs, seven were elected from Jammu and two from Kashmir.

Reservation for women in Panchayats in J&K, as already stated, is quite a late development. By an amendment in the J&K Panchayati Raj Act, 33% seats at the panchayat level were reserved for women. As a result, 2011 elections saw a huge number of woman panchs in the state. A total of 9,424 women were elected as panchs, which was a big change compared to the small number of women elected during the 2001 election. Since the reservation was provided for the first time, most of the woman candidates were freshers in politics as well as in public life. Mostly, women were proxy candidates for the men in their family. Where men could not contest due to their constituency being reserved, they persuaded the women in their families to contest the election – usually the wife, but also mothers and other female relatives.

Unfortunately, the provision of reservation for women was confined to the level of village panchayats only and the principle was not applied to the level of sarpanch. So very few women sarpanchs could be elected. Of the total 4,053 sarpanchs in the state, only 28 were women. Of these twenty-eight women sarpanchs, twenty-five were elected in Jammu division and only three women sarpanchs could be elected in Kashmir.

Despite having panchayats in J&K for the last two decades, the grassroots democratisation has remained a distant dream in this part of the country. The Panchayati Raj Act of 1989 continued lacking in many crucial aspects. The Act has undergone many changes in recent years. By the Jammu and Kashmir Panchayati Raj Amendment Act 2014, one-third sarpanch constituencies have been reserved for women. So, in the latest panchayat elections held in 2018, a large number of women sarpanchs were elected.

The state also witnessed the first ever elections for the Block Development Council in 2019. Though the elections were indirect as the incumbent panchs and sarpanchs of the respective blocks voted for the chairpersons of the Block Development Council, one-third of the seats were reserved for women including SC/ST women. The same principle has been applied for the newly established District Development Councils. By a recent Order for the Union Territory, provision was made for direct election of DDCs and provision was also made for reservation of 33% constituencies for women. What was significant about this election was that the principle of reservation was applied; so, of all the elected members of DDC and Chairpersons, one-third were women.

Women in Urban Local Bodies

The urban local governance in J&K dates back to 1886 when municipalities of Jammu and Srinagar were constituted via the First Municipal Act. The Municipal Act of 1886, as amended in 1889, was replaced by the Jammu and Kashmir Municipal Regulation Act of 1913, thereby introducing elected members and granting the power to levy taxes to these bodies. The 1913 Act was replaced by the J&K Municipal Act of 1941 which tried to strengthen the Act financially. Post-Independence, there have been attempts by the state government to establish bodies of urban governance by promulgating the J&K Municipal

Act in 1951 and to vest more administrative and financial powers to these bodies by amending it in 1956. Finally, the 74th Constitutional Amendment Act of 1992, which granted constitutional status to bodies of urban governance, prompted the State Legislature to enact the Jammu and Kashmir Municipal Act of 2000, replacing the 1951 Municipal Act and the Jammu and Kashmir Municipal Corporation Act of 2000. These Acts drew inspiration from the 74th Constitutional Amendment Act, and hence tried to establish the Municipal Bodies on a fresh pattern so that they could emerge as better instruments of urban self-government.

The two enactments of 2000 restructured the whole system of municipal governance in the state. The Municipalities of Srinagar and Jammu were upgraded to the rank of Corporations, the Town Area Committees were renamed as Municipal Councils, and the Notified Area Committees were renamed as Municipal Committees. The elections to these bodies under the respective Acts were held for the first time in the state in 2005 and thereafter in 2018. There are two Municipal Corporations, six Municipal Councils and seventy-one Municipal Committees in the state. Although, due to the special status of the state, the provisions of 74th Amendment Act could not be extended to J&K, but one-third positions had been reserved for women in all the three levels of the bodies for urban governance in both the Jammu and Kashmir Municipal Act 2000 as well as the Jammu and Kashmir Municipal Corporation Act 2000. Hence, in 2005 as well as in 2018, women took part in the elections to the urban bodies in large numbers and participated actively in urban governance thereafter. In 2018 election only, out of a total 1145 wards, 90 wards had been reserved for Scheduled Castes and 38 wards for Scheduled Tribes which included 31 and 13 wards reserved for SC and ST women respectively. In addition to that, 322 wards had been reserved for women belonging to open category. Hence, one can imagine the scale of emancipation that these bodies of urban governance could ascribe to the aspiring women of urban areas.

The elections for urban bodies are conducted on party basis. So, the political parties reasonably try to encourage women to take part in political activities and impart information as well as support to them. The Women's Wings of almost all political parties have a greater role in this regard. Women candidates fielded by national and regional parties get a wider support base in these elections which adds to their advantage in more ways than one. In fact, the woman Corporators and Councillors have been quite successful in delivering the services in their respective wards. The woman representatives of the urban bodies, having ground knowledge of the genuine situation and problems, have played a very proactive role in addressing the concerns of their areas. Hence, the very provision of reservation has the immense potential to provide tremendous opportunities and the much-required training ground to the women in the field of politics. Moreover, women not only acquire leadership skills but also sincerely work towards the community after getting into these roles. The only limitation seems the absence of continuity of these institutions in the state.

Women and Conflict Politics

Jammu and Kashmir has been embroiled in the conflict situation right since 1947. The conflict itself is complex and has both external as well as internal dimensions. The external dimension of conflict, mainly manifested in the hostility between India and Pakistan, has a long history that starts from the very moment of Accession or even before that when tribesmen from the NWFP (North-West Frontier Province), supported by Pakistan, invaded Jammu and Kashmir. It was the result of the tribal invasion and later the first war between India and Pakistan that the state of Jammu and Kashmir got divided; while the larger part became part of the Indian Union, a smaller part came under the control of Pakistan. The conflict was internationalised as India took the matter to the United Nations. Over the period, India and Pakistan have fought many wars, and borders of Jammu and Kashmir have been severely impacted. Meanwhile, even during the so-called peace time, the border areas have continued to be vulnerable due to the intermittent shelling and firing. It is only few exceptional times, for instance between 2003-2009 (and also after 2021), that the guns have actually fallen silent in the border areas.

Wars and border skirmishes have made the life of people living on the border quite difficult – besides facing shelling, firing, mining and fencing, they have been faced with the problem of multiple displacement. Apart from the border clashes, the armed militancy that overtook the state in the last three decades has impacted the people on a large scale. Though it was the Kashmir Valley that was completely overtaken by the militancy and separatist politics in the 1990s, it had its severe implications on many parts of Jammu region as well. While militarisation and violence impacted people in a variety of ways, this phenomenon also led to large-scale displacements, including the near-complete exodus of Kashmiri Pandits from the Kashmir Valley. The period of militancy saw the killing of a large number of people, abductions, sexual crimes and disruptions of various kinds. In this whole situation, Kashmir has remained the central point – the theatre of conflict and it is here that the maximum impact of conflict can be seen. Apart from the day-to-day disruptions to normal life, there have been prolonged agitations leading to breakdown of normalcy. There have been many other implications of the conflict on people including large-scale violence and militarisation.

The protracted conflict and its multiple dimensions have impacted the people in a variety of ways; and as it happens in any conflict, the most devastating impact of conflict is felt by women and children. The conclusions drawn by a study conducted by UNIFEM (United Nations Development Fund for Women) and UNDP (United Nations Development Programme) can be equally applied to Jammu and Kashmir. This study noted various consequences of conflict situation for women including, 'forced displacements, deaths of close relatives and primary breadwinners, loss of employment, destruction of homes and agricultural lands, prolonged curfew, and the lack of proper health services' (Eileen Kuttab and Riham Barghouti, 2002).

Conflict adds to the vulnerability of women. What is ironic is that the vulnerability that women face is not only because of others but even their own people. Their vulnerability makes them fall victim to exploitation from various sides. The impact of conflict on women takes different forms depending on the nature of conflict and the nature of the social and cultural context in which women are placed. However, despite the internal differentiation and different implications of conflict for different situations of women, gender as a category operates in conflict. Sexual violence has been noted to be the most visible form of violence against women. With stigma being attached to sexual crimes in most societies, it then has other implications for women. As Chenoy[29] notes,

> Besides the social stigma, the incident of rape is further used to restrict the freedom and mobility of women. Once

---

29 Anuradha M Chenoy has been a professor at the School of International Studies, Jawaharlal Nehru University, Delhi. She has written and published widely on international relations from the gender perspective.

> such a situation develops in which women are seen to be vulnerable, the community's response towards women changes. Consequently, a new kind of conservatism surges in the society. Because of fear of being raped, women are forced to remain inside and are not allowed anywhere without a male consort.
>
> (Chenoy, 2002, 132)

Women in the conflict situation also often end up with the responsibility of managing the family singlehandedly. Separation from their men folk, death of family members and loss of livelihood therefore remain constant issues for women in the conflict situation (Chenoy, 2002, 132).

Apart from sexual violence, there are many other specific implications of conflict on women. Of these, displacement is the most significant one. Displacement though difficult for both men and women, leads to specific hardships for women. The most vulnerable among women face the severest implications of displacement due to the conflict situation. As Butalia[30] notes,

> Most affected in the process of displacement are the old women who are forced to live in isolation. They are imprisoned in their places of living. Women also bear the burden of emotional crisis due to lack of education, health facility, forced idleness and unemployment.
>
> (Butalia, 2002, xiii)

30 Urvashi Butalia is an Indian feminist writer, publisher and activist. She is known for her work in the women's movement of India, as well as for authoring several books. She is also the co-founder of 'Kali for Women', India's first feminist publishing house. Later she founded Zubaan Books.

Rita Manchanda, an established writer, scholar-researcher, and human rights activist specialising in conflicts and peace-building in South Asia, refers to 'cultural violence' as an implication of the conflict situation. 'In violent conflict,' she notes, 'cultural violence against women gets magnified. Various cultural taboos are introduced against women and they are forced to step back into the four walls of domesticity and face various limitations on their freedom' (Manchanda, 2001, 70-72).

Women, however, are not just the victims of the conflict situation. They may be also involved on the side of the combatants. Despite the fact that women are the worst sufferers of conflict, it is important to point out that women are also involved in the conflict situation in a number of ways. As part of the community engaged in the conflict situation, they may be identifying and sympathising with the side to which they belong, they may be supporting the combatants explicitly, and even taking up more active roles. Since women are very much linked with their family and have strong community bonds, they are part of the political socialisation and are mobilised in favour of the political 'cause' being followed by the community. Hence, it may be erroneous to categorise the response of women in an apolitical manner and assume that while men make war, women are passive recipients of the conflict situation and are dragged into it absolutely involuntarily. The gender context of conflict however is more nuanced and should be therefore seen in a manner in which one can make fine distinctions. It may be possible that the roles that are assigned within the conflict situation may be gendered with men being at the centre of conflict politics. There may be a disproportionately larger number of men visible in the public space and very few women may be seen as actors. This may be more true of the decision-making positions which may be mostly dominated by men with a rarity of women being visible in that situation. However, the involvement of women may be there in a variety of ways.

Women may be active in violence as many examples of women combatants can be cited, especially in prolonged conflict situations. The case of LTTE (Liberation Tigers of Tamil Eelam) in Sri Lanka where women were actively involved as combatants and part of the suicide squads can be cited in this context. Various roles played by women in this conflict situation are analysed by Vidyamali Samarasinghe, a well-known expert in the area of gender in developing countries who has authored several books.[31] She highlights the agency of women in this situation and refers to two mutually supportive categories, i.e. situational and strategic. Situational category includes private roles like life sustainer, life savers, life givers, and even victimhood. Whereas strategic category includes women's role in relation to war like soldiers, martyred mothers and peace makers (Samarasinghe, 2012). To quote Rita Manchanda,

> Beyond the icon of Mother Sorrow, there are many faces of women in conflict situations in South Asia. Women have negotiated conflict situation by becoming citizens, combatants, heads of households, war munitions workers,

---

31 Samarasinghe's research explores gender in Southeast Asia, female sex trafficking, women's work around the world, and the impact that conflict has on women.

> prostitutes, producers of soldiers and war resisters and political leaders at local and national level. In South Asia, at one end, is the Women of Violence represented by the Armed Virgin of the LTTE, at the other end is the Woman of Peace, symbolised by the Naga Mothers Association (NMA) in the nationalist struggle for an independent Nagaland.
>
> (Manchanda 2001, 5-9)

There is therefore a need to acknowledge the agency of women and their multiple roles in conflict situation. It is also important to acknowledge that conflict has mixed implications for women. Apart from the negative implications of conflict because of vulnerability of women, there is also the possibility that conflict situation may loosen the strict hold of tradition and patriarchal culture and make way for women to move beyond their gender-confined roles. With men engaged in militarised operations, women may be forced into the public space, which might be a near impossibility in the normal times.

This new understanding about the implications of the conflict situation has reflected on women from different angles. Beyond victimisation, there is now a search for women's agency, their techniques of survival and coping and even their role in the peace process.

Turbulence in 1947: Beginning of Conflict in J&K

If one has to trace the history of conflict in Jammu and Kashmir and its impact on women there, one has to go back to the period of partition in 1947, specifically when the state witnessed internal turbulence and was raided by the tribesmen.

Unlike other princely states of India, J&K state did not accede either to India or Pakistan by 15 August 1947. Maharaja Hari Singh, the ruler of the state, sought standstill agreement both from India and Pakistan. While Pakistan agreed immediately, India was still considering it when trouble started. Along with an internal rebellion in the areas of Poonch and Mirpur, there was a tribal invasion. It was due to the combined effect of the internal rebellion and the tribal invasion that a large part of the state came under the control of Pakistan. The end point of this situation was that the state stood divided. While the larger part of this state remained on the Indian side, a substantial part was separated and came under the control of Pakistan. The division, like elsewhere, led to large-scale migration, displacement and killings. After the accession of the state with India, Indian armed forces got engaged in liberating parts of the state and thereafter the first war between India and Pakistan started. However, as the ceasefire came into effect on 1 January 1949, a large part of the state was still under the occupation of Pakistan. The division of the state, being marked by a transitory border (the Ceasefire Line which was later termed as the Line of Control), has had huge implications for the people of this erstwhile princely state.

The most reported communal violence in J&K during 1947 was the 'Jammu Massacre' of Muslims. There have been several reports of a large number of Muslims being killed in Jammu. Most of these reports refer to a change in the demography of Jammu region and its transformation from a Muslim-majority region to a Hindu-majority region. While the actual figures of the Muslims killed during this time vary, the whole episode has been embroiled in controversy. Though in Jammu side, there has been a total silence on these killings, on the Kashmir side, there has been a selective mention of only Muslim killings without any reference to Hindu killings.

Violence was an overarching phenomenon that impacted both Muslims and Hindus. While a large number of Muslims were killed in Jammu, a large number of Hindus were killed as well. We have already made reference to the tribal invasion which resulted in similar atrocities being committed against Hindus. The impact of such communal killings was felt after peace was established. It is not only the Jammu region on the Indian side that saw demographic changes, but the demography of the area under Pakistan's control also changed drastically. The towns and villages in that area became totally bereft of any Hindu population. In both the cases, the change in demography was the result of violence and migration of people.

The communal violence in Jammu region has been much talked about but not properly analysed. A large number of Muslims were killed in the towns of Jammu, Kathua, Samba, Reasi, and Udhampur (Bose, 2003, 40).[32] However, much before these killings, the overall environment of the region was affected by communal politics involving the Muslim

32 Sumantra Bose has been a Professor of International and Comparative Politics at the London School of Economics and Political Science. He has worked extensively on conflict and peace in Jammu and Kashmir.

Conference, Muslim Militia, the RSS and Hindu Mahasabha. The social milieu was quite heavily impacted by rumours, mutual suspicions, insecurities and apprehensions. While the Muslims suspected that Hindus were getting ready to strike them, the Hindus were apprehensive that Muslims were grouping to take some action.

Much before the violence, Jammu had become a transit point for the Hindu and Muslim refugees using the area for reaching safe places – Hindus and Sikhs coming from west Punjab towards East Punjab and Muslims fleeing East Punjab going towards West Punjab. Om Saraf, a leading Jammu journalist and eminent intellectual of the region, was a personal witness to the 1947 events. He has noted how the people affected by partition violence were getting in contact with the local people and affecting the environment of Jammu region. There was also linkage of this violence with the communal developments that had been taking place in the region for quite some time, not only in the plains of Jammu but also in the Pothwari belt of Poonch and Mirpur. Choudhary[33] argues that much before the communal violence broke out in Jammu province in November 1947, this belt had already been severely polarised on communal lines and 'some of the violence in Jammu province was in eruption months before – as early as March-April'. The anti-Dogra movement that had been taking

33 Zafar Choudhary is a Jammu-based journalist, author, policy analyst, and practitioner of peace-building. He was founding editor of *Epilogue*, a monthly journal focusing on J&K. At present, he is the Chief Editor of *The Dispatch*, an online digital news service.

place in this belt had 'assumed communal connotations leading to massive migration of Hindus and Sikhs – mostly influential businessmen – into Jammu city, its peripheral areas, and also into the eastern Punjab (Choudhary, 2012, 34).' It was in this situation of increasing communal polarisation that violence in Punjab and the resultant migration – of Hindus from Sialkot and Muslims from Jammu to Sialkot – set the stage for the excessive communal violence in the region.

It was in this environment that a large number of Muslims were killed in different parts of the region (in Jammu, Udhampur, Reasi, Kathua) around the last week of October 1947 (Choudhary, 2012, 39). One does not know the actual number of Muslims and Hindus killed during the 1947 violence. Christopher Snedden who has analysed the 1947 violence in Jammu region notes that though research is required to confirm the number of Muslims killed, but a large number of Muslims were killed. Many more migrated towards Pakistan or towards the area under the control of Pakistan. To quote him, 'Certainly, a large number of Jammu Muslims, around 400,000, also fled to Pakistan or to the newly-found Azad Kashmir, which had about 150,000 refugees… (Snedden, 2017, 167).' He goes on to note further that there was similar killing and migration of Hindus:

> While the violence against Muslims in eastern Jammu Province was alarming, Muslims in western parts of the province concurrently engaged in similar diabolical acts. In Mirpur District and the Poonch Jagir, Muslims killed large number of Hindus and Sikhs, raped and/or abducted females,

> or forced non-Muslims to flee either to Hindu dominant parts of Jammu Province or to India. By 1951, of the former approximately 114,000 non-Muslims who in 1941 had lived in areas that later came to comprise Azad Kashmir… only a paltry 790 non-Muslims remained.
>
> (Snedden, 2017, 167)

The invasion started on 22 October 1947 with a major attack on Muzaffarabad. As Whitehead notes, the invasion was staged with a clear motive to 'forestall Kashmir's accession to India… They had been encouraged by some of their religious leaders… sections of Pakistan's government and armed forces provided more tangible support in the form of trucks, fuel and rifles and a few key personnel (Whitehead, 2021, 195-212).' Thus, Whitehead reports, the tribesmen from NWFP, 'many of them Mahsuds and Afridis, crossed into the princely state, seized control of the town of Muzaffarabad and advanced east along the Jhelum valley road towards Baramulla and Srinagar.'

The story of the Muzaffarabad attack has been documented by Krishna Mehta in her book, *Kashmir 1947: A Survivor's Story (2006).* As she notes, the tribesmen committed a lot of excesses against the people, indulged in killings, looting and committing sexual crimes against women. There was large-scale violence in which the Hindus and Sikhs were killed; a large number had to evacuate and seek refuge in other parts of the state.

After the Muzaffarabad carnage, the tribesmen reached Baramulla and indulged in looting and killing. While the Sikhs,

Hindus and Christians were targeted, even the local Muslims were not spared by them. There are indications that women were raped also (Whitehead, 2021). There were many local supporters of National Conference who were trying to defend the town from the invasion. The most prominent among these was Maqbool Sherwani who tried to misguide them for almost three days, and was later captured and mercilessly killed.

The extent of the initial tribal invasion was so large that it affected the whole of Pir Panjal range. Besides Muzaffarabad, the towns of Bhimbar, Rajouri, Mendhar, Thanamandi, Darhal, Budhal, Surankote, Bagh, Rawalakot, Mirpur and Kotli were some of the other towns on this range that came under the control of the tribesmen (*The Dispatch Staff*, 2018). Of all these areas, only the story of Poonch and Mirpur has been somewhat documented. These two towns which had a large Hindu and Sikh population, were only liberated months after being under siege. Mirpur city, that was the district headquarter of Mirpur district, was attacked on 24 November and witnessed a massive carnage that lasted for days together. The city which had an average population of 15,000 had a surge in its population due to influx of Hindus and Sikhs from west Punjab and the villages around Mirpur. Despite the fact that the Muslims mostly deserted the city soon after the arrival of the tribesmen, it is estimated that at the time, the population of Mirpur was around 25,000. As per Bal Gupta (2011), a Mirpur survivor who has written his memoir (*Forgotten Atrocities: Memoirs of a Survivor of the 1947 Partition of India*), around 15,000 people were killed. The local people tried to offer resistance with the help of the locally stationed Dogra forces but such resistance could not last for long. The problems for people became complicated as Rao Rattan Singh, the Deputy Commissioner of Mirpur quietly deserted and left for Jammu. As per the available narratives, 2000 people were captured and killed after being brought to a place named Kasgumma. Another group of 2000 people were brought to Thathal; they also met the same fate. A large group of people were brought to Alibeg Gurudwara which was turned into a prison. While many of these were killed, around 1600 prisoners of Alibeg were saved by the ICRC (International Committee of Red Cross) team in January 1948. They were exchanged later in lieu of Muslim prisoners who wanted to go to the Pakistan side (Gupta, 2020).

Like Mirpur, there was a siege of Rajouri town as well. Amar Nath Saraf (2007) has written a personal memoir of the siege of Rajouri. Like in the other places, Hindus from the surrounding villages had located themselves in the town. From October 1947 to April 1948, the town remained under siege. As per personal witnesses, while some Hindus fearing the attack had managed to escape from the town, many others were massacred.

Impact of Violence on Women

How were women located during the turbulence of 1947? The only documentation that is available for this period is about the 'women's militia' that was formed by the National Conference to fight the tribesmen in Kashmir. Other than that, there is not much systematic documentation about the communal massacres that took place in Jammu region and the dislocation that was faced by people in large numbers. However, there are some references and some personal accounts that give us an impression about the situation. One can see the impact that the turbulence had on women. Women were victimised in a number of ways. Whether the women belonged to the Muslim community or the Hindu community, they faced similar kinds of violence and insecurities. While a large number of them were killed along with their men folk, their gendered existence resulted in added miseries – sexual abuse being the most crucial one. While men of 'other community' were targeted for killing, women were targeted for sexual gratification. While many were sexually abused and killed, many others were seen as part of the 'loot' and were abducted and taken along. At the end of the situation, countless women were separated from their close kin. Later, many women on both the sides were exchanged, however, 'honour' of women became a major issue; and so even when they were reunited, they were not necessarily integrated with their families in a smooth manner.

Krishna Mehta (2006) in her story mentions how she had to escape from her home along with her six children while her husband, Duni Chand Mehta, the Deputy Commissioner of Muzaffarabad, was killed. Mehta has written a complex story comprising not only of killing, abduction, looting and treachery but also of goodwill and kindness of people. Even as she tells the tale of how some people known to her turned into greedy betrayers, she talks about simple and poor people who helped her family despite their poverty and their own problems. In her story, one finds a clear narrative of how women suffered and feared sexual violence and abduction; how many of them committed or tried to commit suicide. She narrates a situation where even she tried to commit suicide.

Reference has also been made about the violence faced by women in the town of Baramulla. The most referred to and reported case is that of the nuns in St Joseph Hospital, Baramulla. The testimony of Rev Father Shanks, who was the principal of St Joseph Degree College in Baramulla and an eye witness to the carnage, has been reproduced by European Foundation for South Asian Studies (EFSAS). As per this testimony:

> The tribesmen – great, wild, black beasts they were – came shooting their way down from the hills on both sides of the town. They climbed over the hospital walls from all sides. The first group burst into a ward firing at the patients. A twenty-year-old Indian nurse, Philomena, tried to protect a Muslim patient whose baby had just been born. She was shot dead first. The Patient was next. Mother Superior Aldetrude rushed into the ward, knelt over Philomena and was at once attacked and robbed. The Assistant Mother, Teresalina, saw a tribesman point a rifle at Mother Aldetrude and jumped in front of her. A bullet went through Teresalina's heart. At the moment Colonel Dykes, who had assured us we would not be attacked, raced from his room a few yards along the terrace to get the Mother Superior out of danger, shouting at the tribesmen as he ran. But the Mother Superior fell shot, and Colonel Dykes collapsed beside her with a bullet in the

> stomach. Mrs Dykes ran from her husband's room to help him. She too was shot dead.
>
> (EFSAS, 2020)

A large number of women were abducted during this time. The tribesmen, while returning, took back with them a large number of women. In a recent BBC report, Ilyas Khan interviewed some tribesmen who were part of the attacking force. He notes how the tribesmen mistreated women and brought back with them many 'enslaved' women. Referring to their treatment of non-Muslims, he notes that, 'They shot everyone who couldn't recite the *Kalima*... Many non-Muslim women were enslaved, while many others jumped in the river to escape capture (Ilyas Khan, 2017).' He talks about how women were part of the booty that they looted. Referring to one of his sources, he cites the son of one of the tribesmen who had gone for the invasion, 'They brought back war booty though; gold and some women.' Referring to this booty, another source claimed, 'Some had brought cattle, some horses. Most of them had brought arms, and many brought women. One Afridi tribesman walked back with two women in tow. They wept incessantly and just wouldn't stop (Khan, 2017).'

In such a situation of uncertainty and chaos, many women committed suicide. Fearing sexual atrocities and abduction, many women took the step of killing themselves by taking poison, or falling into rivers. In many cases, this happened in a collective manner in the presence of family members. With loss of 'honour' being perceived as a major issue by the communities, there was generally a consensus that it was better for women to lose their life rather than lose their 'honour' after being sexually assaulted by men of a different community. That is why there were repeated incidents of such suicides by women. Krishna Mehta (2006) in her narrative tells how committing suicide was always a real option for her while escaping from Muzaffarabad. She narrates a particular incident where she had been summoned by some Muslim officers. Though later she was helped by these very officers, but initially suspecting that she might be sexually victimised, she made an unsuccessful attempt to kill herself.

One of the major incidents of mass suicide of women took place in Rajouri when it was attacked by the tribal forces. Understanding that they would not be able to defend themselves from falling into the hands of enemy forces, many women took their own life. To quote Mohita Bhatia,[34]

> In the context of siege and attack of Rajouri, most widely held narrative…is about the night of Diwali (10 November 1947) when Hindus in Rajouri town, including those who had gathered from far flung villages, were assembled in 'Maidaan' (referring to the present main airfield ground in the town) and killed…. In the apprehension of an impending attack, many Hindus tried to escape from Rajouri. Many who failed to escape attempted to kill themselves and their women folk

---

34 Mohita Bhatia is an Assistant Professor in the Department of Sociology at Saint Mary's University, Halifax. She has published articles in various books and journals. Her most recent work is *Rethinking Conflict at the Margins: Dalits and Borderland Hindus in Jammu and Kashmir* (Cambridge University Press, 2020).

> by poisoning or stabbing them. Women drowned themselves in the river and wells to escape sexual harassment and killing at the hands of the tribesmen.
>
> (Bhatia, 2019)

The women who were abducted, and the women who got separated and were left behind, now form the Hindu-Muslim divided families. For a long time, there remained a silence on the abducted or separated women. The tragedy of facing the loss of the women was overcome by the feeling of 'shame'. The dominant belief was that women should be killing themselves rather than falling in the hands of members of the other community in order to save the honour of the family and the community, so the relatives remained silent and did not refer to them for decades together. What happened to these women, is a question that needs to be asked. 'There was no trace of the majority of them. Few others got converted to Islam and had established their families there on the other side of the border (Jamwal and Suchismita, 2012).' It was only after the initiation of peace process and opening of the LoC for the purpose of travel in 2005, that many stories emerged of such women who were left behind across the LoC. Invariably these women had converted to Islam. Many of these women contacted their relatives and could finally meet and visit them. One such story was that of Satya Devi who was separated from her family; she later converted, became Fatima and got married. She could get connected with her sister Kesro Devi seven decades later. They met each other through the internet (Farooq, 2018).

Inderjit Kaur's story is a similar tragic tale. She got left behind on PoK side. She married a Muslim youth known to the family and within a year gave birth to a girl. But later, in 1948, due to her brother's efforts, Inderjit was reunited with her parents in India, but she was separated from her infant daughter. After more than five decades, Inderjit was able to meet her daughter Bi Behum, living in Kotli district of PoK, due to the efforts of Yuv Raj Gupta, a central government employee, in the backdrop of the Indo-Pak peace process (One India, 2006).

Other than losing their home and relatives, these women also suffered the loss of their identity. They had to accept a new religion, a new name and a new nation. And their dilemmas about their identity continued to remain with them even when they could finally meet their relatives. Referring to these women, Anuradha Bhasin Jamwal notes that many 'are living with dual identity although not out of choice, as the same was thrust upon them by the whims of some and quirk of fate' (Jamwal and Suchismita, 2012).

Continued Implications of Conflict in Post-1947 Period

The trauma of people in Jammu and Kashmir, especially the people living around the borders, didn't end with the turbulence in 1947. The border people were now a new category reflecting the marginality and continued struggle of their day-to-day life. Within this broad category, two more categories were created – the 'displaced' and the 'divided' families. The displaced known as PoK refugees were the Hindu natives who were forced to migrate from various towns and villages that came under the control of Pakistan in 1947. Having lost their homes, land and livelihood in PoK, they were forced to start their lives afresh. Since the areas from where they were displaced was still claimed by India to be its part, these displaced people could not be formally recognised as Pakistani refugees and were not rehabilitated at par with Pakistani refugees from Punjab and Bengal. With meagre support from the state, they struggled for decades to rehabilitate themselves. For women among these refugees, it was certainly a tough life. Without the comfort of their homes, they had to provide for the basic necessities of their children. Many of them shared the economic burden by doing odd jobs, thereby extending the sphere of their responsibilities.

Apart from these displaced people, the division of the state resulted in the division of families also. With the abrupt drawing of the border (the Line of Control), they lost contact with part of their families. One may quote Bhasin Jamwal to elaborate this phenomenon of divided families:

> The unnatural line demarcates boundaries between India and Pakistan, especially the bloody LoC cuts through mountains, often slicing a village into two halves with people living side by side, sharing the same address in terms of the name of village but different nationalities; many families divided by a cruel twist of politics and strategic concerns.
>
> (Jamwal and Suchismita, 2012)

Due to the stringent border control, these families lost all contact with their relatives who were living across the Line of Control. There are many stories of people desperately desiring to meet their close relatives, being not allowed to do so, and passing away disappointed, as till 2005 there was no easy way for crossing the LoC.

The implications of the bordering process were not limited to these categories of people but extended to all those who were living near the border. The borders have not been peaceful since a long time. While the first major war between India and Pakistan took place as early as October 1947, there have been other wars between these two countries in later periods. There was the war in 1965, then in 1971, then the Kargil War in 1999, and an almost war-like situation arose following the terrorist attack on the Parliament in 2001. These wars apart, there have been constant tensions on the India-Pakistan borders. In fact, with the exception of a brief period of less than a decade after 2003, when a formal ceasefire was agreed upon between India and Pakistan (and since 2021 when the two countries reaffirmed the ceasefire), the borders in Jammu and Kashmir have remained volatile. With the settled border between India and Pakistan known as International Border (IB) and the unsettled border known as LoC crossing through this erstwhile state, a large part of J&K lives on the border, thus the hostilities between India and Pakistan certainly impact a large number of people. During the wars and during the ceasefire violations, even the civilian population gets to be targeted; there are many cases when people on the zero line get killed or seriously injured in the shelling and firing that takes place.[35] To save themselves from this situation, people are also forced to flee their homes at odd hours. Temporary displacement and dislocation is a very common and frequent experience of border people. There are periods when such dislocations are for short durations like a couple of days, and there are other times when it can prolong for months. This dislocation brings a lot of discomfort and disruption in their normal lives and makes them vulnerable and dependent on state support.

Other than the shelling and firing, the people are also affected by the excessive militarisation of the areas where they reside. Often the hostilities lead to the situation of mining the area which includes the agricultural land. During the prolonged mobilisation of forces in 2001, large areas were mined, and as a consequence, people had to abandon their agricultural activities till the time their fields were de-mined. Agriculture also gets affected by the process of fencing. In the last three decades, a lot of agricultural land has come under the areas of fencing because the fence meant to secure borders is located quite inside the border. This means that there are a large number of people who are residing in the fenced areas or whose agricultural land is within the fenced area. Besides affecting their livelihood, this

35 To quote Christophe Jaffrelot, French political scientist and Indologist specialising in South Asia, particularly India and Pakistan, 'The number of ceasefire violations (CFVs) in Kashmir has sharply increased in recent years, and even more dramatically since 2017. India and Pakistan have not fought each other openly since the 1999 Kargil conflict and have oscillated between military tension and peace talks, but the growing number of violations since 2013 threatens to push the countries back to the dangerous posturing of the late 1990s and early 2000s (Jaffrelot, 2018).'

has various other implications for the people living there since movement inside the fenced areas is quite restricted. The areas are not only under the constant watch of the security forces, but also any movement within them is possible only with their explicit permission.

Living on the border has a lot of implications for women. The intermittent firing on the border does affect their normal lives and they have to remain extra cautious about the safety of their families. In the villages near the zero line, the houses come in the firing range which often leads to injury or even death of people. While agricultural activities get adversely affected, women are restrained from going to the fields. Even so they have to cater to their animals. As per the gender division of labour, taking care of farm animals and poultry is the responsibility of women. They therefore face the hazards of firing and shelling on a regular basis. One can cite a number of recent examples of women having suffered due to border firing. In July 2020, a woman Resham Bi was killed and another woman Hakim Bi was injured when there was cross-border firing in Lanjote area of Mendhar. These women, as per news reports, were trying to shift their cattle from an open veranda to a shed. A mortar shell that fell within their house resulted in the killing and injury (Scroll, 2020). During another incident in November 2020, a woman suffered splinter injuries when two shells exploded in the compound in Manyari village in Kathua district. In yet another incident, two women Mansha Bi and Sakeena Bi, residents of Bagyal Dara in Dallan Sector of Poonch were injured (*Indian Express*, 2020).

There are many occasions when the intensity of firing so increases that the people have to be evacuated from their homes and villages and are temporarily relocated in safer places nearby. Most of the times, it happens that women and children are sent to safer places and accommodated in public spaces like schools. While women become displaced and are forced to live without the comforts of home for days or even months together, they are made to singlehandedly take on the responsibility of the children and the elders. The lack of privacy in these public spaces makes their lives difficult; it has an adverse effect on their health and psyche. Reflecting on the impact of displacement on women, Bhasin Jamwal thus notes:

> Displacement has changed two major things for the women. The first has to do with the changing economic status, bringing in poverty and deprivation among the set of people who had previously grown enough food on their farms to meet their needs. The second change has to do with taking over the role of managing livelihood for the family while their male counterparts have slipped into acute frustration, depression and alcoholism.
>
> (Jamwal and Suchismita, 2012)

One major issue that women who are living near the zero-line face relates to their agricultural land coming under the fencing. After the onset of militancy, borders have been systematically fenced. However, rather than fencing right on the zero line, it is done much ahead. At certain places, large chunks of agricultural land fall within the fenced area.[36] Such areas are under the strict surveillance of the security forces and people are allowed to do farming only for a limited time during the day. This has had the consequence of alienating women from agricultural activities. In any case, the border villages are highly militarised zones and affect the lives of women in a number of ways. Apart from the restriction in their mobility, there is also an impact on their education. The areas being remote and militarised, women are discouraged from going out of the village for education after a certain level – generally the higher secondary level.

POK Refugees and Divided Families – Implications for Women

As stated above, the abrupt division of the state in the 1947-48 period created many new categories of people. As mentioned, apart from the 'bordered people', at least two new categories came into being – the 'divided families' and the 'refugees'.

The divided families were faced with not only the pain of separation from very close relatives but also from lack of access to travel across the border or even communicate with the separated relatives – in many cases parents, children or siblings. The vulnerability of women with their gendered existence made such pain much more unbearable. Unlike

36 About agricultural land, Ashutosh Sharma writes – 'Farmers in at least 12 villages of Samba district and almost 20 villages in Kathua district have more than 20,358 kanal agricultural land across the fence. Army doesn't allow us to cultivate it. The government doesn't pay us any financial compensation (*National Herald*, 2019).'

men who enjoyed relative freedom in matters of obtaining information, these women were dependent on male members and therefore were relatively more deprived even in terms of obtaining information about their close relatives. The situation was much more difficult in cases of cross-religious divided families. Till very recently, one would not have much information about such families because the concerned women of these families were mainly those who were either abducted or separated from the family during the division of the state in 1947. Mostly, the Hindu and Sikh women who were for any reason separated from the family and left on their own in PoK, eventually married and got converted to Islam. These women faced not only the hazards of separation but also the pain of their families disowning them. In the name of family 'honour', the knowledge about their very existence was totally decimated from within the family so that even the next generation did not have any information about these women having been left behind in PoK. The number of such women must have been quite high because when the cross-LoC travel was opened, there were many such women, now in their old age, seeking contact with their families back in India; and many of them, by their sheer desire to meet their relatives, did visit during this time. One can only imagine the life of these women who were not only separated from their families but also had to accept a new religion and a new nationality.

The refugees, mostly those Hindus who were forced to leave their villages and homes in the now PoK, were relocated in different parts of Jammu region. Since they had to start their lives from scratch, they were faced with many hardships. As the areas from where they were uprooted was claimed to be part of India, they were not properly rehabilitated but were given some help in the form of land to build a home in case of urban refugees and agricultural land for cultivation in case of rural refugees. Mostly, these refugees rehabilitated themselves by their sheer hard work.

Most of the refugees, before being dislocated from their homes, were living a comfortable life. As most of them were either landowners or traders, they were quite prosperous. One hears a lot of stories about the PoK refugees having big houses, orchards, jewellery, cattle and other assets 'back home'. After being relocated in Jammu, they had to build their lives all over again with men mostly taking odd jobs, including that of hawkers, street venders and even labourers. Women had to make do with the lack of resources, scarcities and poor economic situation. Many women who were homebound had to look for odd jobs. As it happens everywhere in a conflict situation, displacement brought additional burdens for women; along with the hazards of relocations which they had to share with the men of the family, they also had to face the situations generated by patriarchy and male dominance. With many families changing their character and losing the support of the extended joint family and community, there was increase in the vulnerability of women with some of them facing domestic tensions and even violence. At the same time, there were also situations where control over women was somewhat loosened as the dislocation had the impact of making flexible many structures of control. Thus the strict distinction of gender roles between the public and private space of home was somewhat toned down as some women had to take up jobs for economic reasons.

The Implications of Militancy on Women

The protracted conflict in Jammu and Kashmir since the late eighties has had multiple implications on women. Since conflict escalates the vulnerability of powerless people, women as the most vulnerable section of society were exposed to the worst kinds of situations – situations of marginalisation, of sexual victimisation, of impoverished state, of single parenthood, of emotional and psychological trauma, etcetera.

What became the major outcome of the conflict in the post-1989 period was the all pervasiveness of the gun. There were multiple sources of violence. The conflict has had such a vast impact that it has affected almost every family. Though the men who were the combatants faced the maximum brunt of violence, conflict also impacted the women. One major implication of the conflict situation in Kashmir was the killing or disappearance of a large number of men and therefore the presence of a large number of widows and 'half-widows'. As these women were mostly uneducated and without much background of working outside the home, the absence of men in the family suddenly brought them face to face with the question of their survival. Sustenance of the family became the primary issue for these women. Women in the rural areas having some land faced somewhat lesser problems, but there were many women who did not have land or any other resource to live by. In many cases, they were dependent on their parental families as the in-laws refused to support them. The only relief that they had in case of Kashmir was that they did not face the psychological burden of 'widowhood' as faced by women elsewhere in India. As Ritu Dewan[37] notes, women in Kashmir don't face the stigma of widowhood and widows get remarried as a normal course. However, for those women who were having children, marriage was a difficult option. In many cases, they chose not to marry because they were not sure that their children would be accepted by the men they married (Dewan, 1994, 2654).

The problems were however different for 'half widows' – the women whose husbands had gone missing and could not be traced for many years. There would be no information as to whether these people were living or dead. Due to the lack of information, their wives were given the uncertain status of 'half widows'. Referring to the phenomenon of 'half widows' in Kashmir, Insha Malik has thus pointed out,

> These women are on their own, helping their families to survive, while dealing with the complicated position of their marital status. They are married and yet not married; it is a chaotic state as the number of such women in Kashmir is really high. Widows in Kashmir are especially hard hit. The

---

37 Ritu Dewan is the Vice President of the Indian Society of Labour Economics; she was the President of the Indian Association for Women's Studies from 2014-17. She has taken keen interest in gender issues emanating from conflict situation in Jammu and Kashmir.

> low status accorded to widows is embedded in Kashmiri society, cutting across class, and for half widows the stigma is even worse. They have to take up the reins of running a family with little or no education. Many have never worked outside their homes before. Moreover, they can neither claim compensation from the government that other widows are entitled to, nor inherit the property of their husbands. In many cases, they have been forced to leave their in-laws house and either return to their parents or try and eke out a living on their own.
>
> (Malik, 2013, 52-53)

Being a 'half widow' had a number of social and legal implications for women. According to the customary law, till such time the death of a man was not confirmed, the woman could not be legally seen as a widow and therefore could not be rehabilitated. The issues related to their remarriage, inheritance of property, compensation – all remained hanging. Due to the failure of religious scholars coming to any conclusion regarding the number of years after which the wife of a missing man could remarry, these women were living a life of uncertainty. More recently, an initiative was taken by local women activists to resolve the issue of the waiting period. They mobilised the clergy and pressed them to reach a consensus on this issue. The Muslim clerics agreed upon a four-year waiting period following the absence of the husband for a woman to remarry.

In the absence of much civil society support to the half-widows, the vacuum has been filled by APDP (Association of

Parents of Disappeared Persons). APDP was organised locally by Parveena Ahangar whose own son had disappeared. It was in the process of searching for her missing son that Parveena launched this organisation to provide support to women like her whose sons or husbands had gone missing during the conflict situation.

Of the various kinds of violence that women were subjected to, sexual violence was the most vicious one. Such violence was committed by all sides – by the state actors as well as non-state actors. As Misri has noted,

> Rape, gang-rape, kidnapping and abductions, which huge numbers of Kashmiri women are subjected to, in the current conflict, are the worst manifestations of sadist macho masculinity. The barbaric acts are related to the patriarchal notions of women being the property of men, and therefore, the physical violations of women amount to challenging the collective 'honour' and 'purity' of communities. Women are targeted primarily to create terror and break the spirit of the 'enemy'. Also, abduction and rape become strategies for stripping women of their personal assets and of their political assets – honour or more precisely community honour.
>
> (Misri, 2010, 315-316).

The issues related to sexual violence are not seen from the perspective of the victimised women but from the perspective of honour of the family and community. To quote Jamwal,

> This 'honour' discourse in rapes has masculine connotations. At one level, the definition of rape as a violation of woman's

> honour and dignity tends to stigmatise the woman and make her psychological ostracisation from society easier. At another level, it is the male honour, hurt and bruised, that tends to take precedence over the suffering and stymie the women's victimisation. It is interesting how this politics of rape and the aftermath proceeds, putting woman in a doubly disadvantageous position, where she seems to be deprived of not just a chance to move on with her life with dignity but also a right to grieve. Victimisation becomes eternal, something even glamorised, contradicting with the syndrome of stigma, in form of protests and documentation of human rights abuse. The victim is forgotten and expected not to exist.
>
> (Jamwal, 2010, 331)

What is peculiar about the sexual violence discourse is that it is politically appropriated without any gender implications. As has been the case in Kashmir, rape remained the central issue in the separatist political discourse, but rather than being seen from the perspective of women, it was seen from the 'political' context. The issue was raised to point out the coercive nature of the state response towards the Kashmiri community. It was also an issue around which the sentiments of the community were invoked. However, the women who faced sexual violence continued to live stigmatised lives; the concern of the political discourse around rape did not extend to dealing with the issue of stigma and isolation of women.

One of the major reasons as to why the gender perspective has been missing in the discourse of rape lies in the absence of women in the political discourse itself. The issue of rape is generally raised from forums which do not have any presence of women. And there is no such women's organisation in Kashmir which speaks from the perspective of women. To quote Jamwal (2010, 330-331),

> It is equally significant to note the response of the civil society in cases of rapes, where women again play a marginal role, and allow the entire discourse of rape to be defined on the parameters of 'outraging modesty' of the woman who is upheld as a symbol of virtues and honour of the male members of her family and community. The near absenteeism of women activism outside the traditional political organizations makes the masculine interpretation of rape and its abuse as a political ploy, the predominant feature.

Conflict, on the whole, resulted in the pervasiveness of the masculinist discourse on the one hand and vulnerability of women on the other. As Nyla Ali Khan says, this resulted in the 'brutalisation of the culture', 'socialisation of Kashmiri boys and men into a military culture' and the already existing hierarchical relationship between men and women getting linked with 'sexualised violence' (Khan, 2009,101).

The impact of brutalisation of culture was noted by many of our respondents during the field study. As per one respondent,

> I come from a fairly good economic background. My father was a businessman and gave us all the freedom and rarely intervened in our activities. We were two sisters and three brothers, and we bonded very well with each other. Till my

> school days, I never felt handicapped as a girl; I could do whatever my brothers did. In fact, my brothers, who were older than me, encouraged us not only to take up non-conventional lines of education but also to participate in sports and cultural activities. Things however changed with the onset of militancy. My mother started insisting that I cover my head while going to college. My brothers started becoming very protective and asking me questions even if I was half an hour late from college.

According to another respondent, a resident of the downtown area,

> As the militancy started, the boys in our locality were very much swayed by it. A number of them quit studies and became active militants. There were others who did not formally join militancy, but became very aggressive supporters of militancy. A few of them also got influenced by the changed religious discourse and changed their life style. They became the watchdogs of the locality and started sending messages to our parents to see to it that we do not dress up or act in an un-Islamic manner.

It was not only the brutalisation of culture that impacted women, but also the overall brutalisation of society.[38] Referring

38 To quote Nyla Ali Khan, 'The brutalization of the culture has been rendered more lethal by the socialization of Kashmiri boys and men into a military culture. Within such a masculinist discourse and praxis, the rigidly entrenched hierarchical relationship between men and women is inextricably linked with sexualized violence (Khan, 2010).'

to the impact of militarisation on the family life of people, Malik noted that brutalisation outside the home led to brutal behaviour within the family. She pointed out a chain effect of militarisation whereby 'the incidence of sexual violence against the women' leads to rage among 'the men in the community' and results in their brutalised response. Malik therefore argued that the reasons for increased domestic violence are to be found in the militarisation of society. Many others argue that Kashmir, which did not have a tradition of domestic violence and other crimes against women, experienced such crimes only in the last few decades. They hold the conflict situation responsible for these.

Both, concern for security of life as well as fear of sexual violence resulted in families restraining the mobility of women. Women themselves felt pressurised not to move openly outside their homes. As a respondent stated,

> During the early period of militancy, we ourselves were constrained and did not feel very safe venturing outside our homes. There was so much of uncertainty over there. No one who went out of the house could be sure that the day would pass uneventfully. There were so many possibilities. One could get struck in the cross fire between the militants and the security forces, one could get injured or killed by sudden explosions on the streets.

Even within the four walls of the house, there was no sense of security. Another respondent said,

> We lost our sense of privacy. During situations of militants striking in the neighbourhood, there were occasions when

> there were crackdowns and we were very scared. There were lots of stories floating at that time about sexual abuse and rape by the security forces. We were terrified when there was such a situation and the men were asked to line up outside and the forces entered our houses.

The conflict situation has affected women across religious lines. Besides the Kashmiri Muslim women, the Kashmiri Pandit women also faced several consequences of the conflict situation. It is important to note that the Kashmiri Pandit community which formed a miniscule but very influential minority left the valley en masse in 1990 in the wake of militancy and mass upsurge. While a large number of them shifted and later settled in Jammu, a large number left for Delhi and other places in India and even outside India (Hans, 2000, 79).[39]

---

39 The exodus was a result of the situation in which Kashmir was placed in the early period of militancy. This was the time when there was an almost complete collapse of the state resulting in a general environment of fear. While there were few killings of prominent Kashmiri Pandits, including that of Justice Ganjoo, Director Doordarshan Lassa Kaul and BJP president of Kashmir and some other notable people – there was a complete disorder. Militancy was also accompanied by mass separatist sentiment that was reflected in the almost daily street demonstrations with slogans of 'azadi'. Finding the situation not conducive to their peaceful survival in Kashmir, there was a mass exodus of Kashmiri Pandits, which started in early March 1990. Referring to the cause of their decision to leave their homes in Kashmir, a women's group that visited them state: 'Some left their homes in the Valley because of fear of Islamisation, some because the pro-Pakistan group Hizbul Mujahideen put up stickers on doors warning them to leave or be killed (Dewan, 1994, 2655).'
As per another woman activist, 'Half a million Hindu families were displaced after loudspeakers broadcasting from mosques asked them to leave the Valley within three day or face dire consequences.' Without much planning and preparation, the Pandits left the valley and their homes without many assets and were mostly located in various migrant camps – tents to begin with, and later one-room tenements (Asha Hans, 2000, 79).

The fear of sexual abuse of women was one of the driving factors in the sudden decision to leave the Valley. The rape and murder of Sarla Bhat, a Kashmiri Pandit nurse of the Sher-e-Kashmir Medical Institute in Soura, created a panic among Hindus who sent their women from the Kashmir Valley to safer places (Hans, 2000A, 22). For many of the displaced Kashmiri Pandits, the threat of sexual abuse had been explicit in the political slogans used at that time. One of the slogans that was most feared by the Pandits was: *Asi gache Pakistan, Batav ros Batnev san* (We want Pakistan, inclusive of Pandit women and exclusive of Pandit men).[40]

The exodus of Kashmiri Pandits affected the community as a whole. While the very context of displacement was psychologically traumatic, they also had to handle several physical challenges. They had to face a lot of hardships not only in terms of their location but also in terms of educational and health facilities. With lack of privacy, the camps were not the most dignified spaces for the Pandits who had lived quite a comfortable life back in Kashmir and had owned multi-storeyed houses there. To quote one respondent in the Nagrota camp: 'We have been cramped up in these one-two rooms – all seven of us; back home, we had a three-storeyed house with twelve rooms.' Privacy and sanitation was a big issue in the

40 However, as Asha Hans notes, it was not only Kashmiri Pandit women but also Kashmiri Muslim women who were forced to leave Kashmir because of militancy. 'They fled for two reasons, fear or economic uncertainty. As to specific reasons for women leaving Kashmir, especially Muslim women, fear of sexual assault by militants and in some cases security personnel has been a major element (Hans, 2000A, 22).'

camp. The following narrative of camp life in Jammu gives a vivid picture of the dismal situation:

> We sought refuge in the migrant quarters at Muthi. These quarters had domes. There were no windows in the damp, dingy room. Perpetual darkness reigned inside our room... We lived for fourteen years in the one-room tenement... The conditions were inhuman.... scorching heat, constricted lanes, mobile water tankers, the din of utensils, long queues for water...a tap of water for 200 families... Not a single day went by without a fight for water.
>
> (Dhar, 2015, 70)

As per another narrative:

> I was born in a one-room tenement... I lived there with my parents for sixteen years.... I spent my childhood in a one-room camp in Muthi. We did everything in that single room. We can now survive in the worst of places... My parents' house in Kupwara was burnt. They sold it some years ago. They told me that ours was a big house surrounded by apple trees.
>
> (Narrative of Sagar Pandita) (Dhar, 2015A 136)[41]

Displaced women had to bear the burden of displacement

---

41 Many of them were not happy with the state dole of 1500 rupees and felt that they had lost their sense of self-respect depending on this dole (Ritu Dewan, 1994, 2655). They were worried about their abandoned houses and had to live with the news of their houses being plundered and burnt. Many of them went in for 'distressed sale' of their houses – getting an insignificantly small amount of money for their property.

in a much more intense manner. They were not only victims of displacement but were faced with specific gender consequences of displacement. They had to leave all that was familiar and secure to adapt to a new life of uncertainty (Asha Hans, 2000, 79).

There were various other social consequences of displacement. Dhingra and Arora in their article 'At the Cross Roads: Families in Distress' state that '...the immediate fallout of migration was very high increase in the number of nuclear families. The traditional joint families were forced to split up due to lack of adequate accommodation... With the collapse of the traditional joint family structure, the support of an integrated family' had gone missing. Dhingra and Arora have also noted the adverse implications of camp life on the self-esteem and marital relations of the Pandits.

> The roles and relationships of the family members have been challenged in the wake of altered living conditions. The male members of the Kashmiri Pandit community are no longer satisfied with the kind of role they are playing these days. They feel that they are no longer capable of taking the responsibility of running their homes, as they do not have good jobs that they had earlier. Government is providing them relief and they are dependent on it. This has produced a feeling of dependence and self-pity... This kind of challenge to their traditional role as providers for their families tends to lead to anger, frustration, uncertainty and helplessness among male members and sometimes this translates into violence against women in the family. Women are facing double stress. Firstly, it is the stress of migration that she has to bear and

> secondly being the weaker sex, she also faces stress in family due to internal tension.
>
> (Dhingra and Arora, 2005, 219-220)

Dhingra and Arora also reported a decline in the birth rate of Pandits.[42] The stress within the family also had a lot of implications for women. Since it is noted that the level of domestic violence increases during conflict situations, instances of increased domestic violence was seen among the displaced also.

---

42 Listing the causes of the decline in birth rate, Dhingra and Arora noted that people do not enjoy marital privacy in the camps. As a result, the birth rate has declined... Other reasons responsible for the fall in population are premature menopause in women, hypo-function of reproductive system, delayed reproduction or infertility, malnutrition, sunstroke and snakebite (Dhingra and Arora, 217-222).

Conflict Politics and Agency of Women

Women's Agency

'Agency refers to the ability to act or perform an action. In contemporary theory, it hinges on the question of whether individuals can freely and autonomously initiate action, or whether the things they do, are in some sense determined by the ways in which their identity has been constructed (Ashcroft, Griffiths and Tiffin, 2004.)'

Agency is linked with the freedom of human beings as well as their competence to make informed choices that matter to their lives. However, it is not only at the individual levels that the term 'agency' is used, it may be exercised at the collective levels as well. As Sabina Alkire, Oxford-based academician, notes, 'Agency may be exercised at the individual level or in groups, or through democratic participation (2005, 217-260).'

It is in more recent times that in the context of conflict, the concept of 'agency' has come in vogue. Generally, the gender binary has been used to locate men and women in the conflict situation.[43] With conflict being associated with masculinity and peace with women, men have been seen to be the initiators and actors in conflict politics, while women have been seen as its mute recipients – as victims, sufferers. In fact, it is not only the conflict, but the whole politics that has been seen from this perspective of gender binary and many of the political concepts have gendered connotations. However, gender studies have gone beyond these traditional notions and have sought to see the complex character of conflict in which women are not merely seen as the silent victims but are also seen in various other roles (Ashcroft, Griffiths and Tiffin, 2004). As the real situation of conflict has been analysed, attention has been placed on various other dimensions of women's participation in conflict politics – thus they are viewed as active actors, perpetrators, sympathisers, helpers, etcetera. Many studies have shown women to be equally politicised and playing key roles in conflict politics.

It is suggested in recent studies that women have their own ways to locate themselves in conflict. They may not be

43 While it is important to focus on the victimisation of women in the conflict situation, but by reducing all gender-angles of conflict to victimisation, one falls into the trap of reinforcing the gender-binaries and stereotypes. It is important to note that victimisation is a reality of the conflict situation. Not only women, men also become victims of conflict. However, due to the structural prevalence of patriarchy, women are weighed down by the double burden of conflict as well as patriarchy. However, referring to women only as victims reinforces the patriarchal structures. With men being placed at the centre stage of conflict, the whole context of women's response and role in conflict is not only marginalised but made instrumental to masculinist discourse of conflict.

emulating men, but in their own ways, have a significant role in conflict politics. To quote Moser and Clark (2005,5):

> For women as much as for men, the experience of violent conflict, as with social life, is not built upon a single discourse. As social actors, they face alternative ways of formulating their objectives, however restricted their resources. The strategies and cultural constructions they employ are drawn from a stock of available discourses (verbal and non-verbal) that are shared with other individuals and contemporaries. Rather than simply being synonymous with individuals, acts are 'socially' constructed in the light of social relations and their environments.[44]

Since their response follows their gendered construction, women may have different positions, perceptions and responses in conflict politics compared to men. To see and analyse these responses, it is important to visualise them from the gender lens. This gender lens will show us that women are not passive spectators in conflict politics and exercise their agency one way or the other.

To argue that women have agency in conflict situation does not mean that there is no victimisation of women. In every conflict, women as well as men are victimised, and the victimisation of women is intensified due to their gendered location. However, to reduce the whole situation of women

---

44 Moser, Caroline ON and Fiona C Clark (eds.), 2005, Victims, *Perpetrators or Actors? Gender, Armed Conflict and Political Violence*, Zed Books.

in conflict politics to that of 'victims', takes away their own 'political' positions and their capacity to act in their own rights. It is in this context that one can refer to Sudha Ramachandran's argument in the South Asian context:

> Women bear the major burden of the violence in conflict areas. However, to regard them just as passive victims would be obscuring their role as agents of change. Whether through passive resistance or protest, active combat or peace building, women in South Asia's conflict areas are slowly emerging from the sidelines. Yet, the fact that they have to function in a highly militarised environment is impeding the pace and extent to which they can determine the direction in which politics and social change will move.
>
> (Ramachandran, 2005, 155)[45]

Various conflict situations at the global level clearly show that there is a collective response of the political community, and women and men are collectively politicised in the conflict politics. With politics being at the centre of conflict, women can't remain untouched and adopt 'apolitical' positions. So women are as much 'political' as the men are. It may be possible that women might be approaching the situation from a different 'political' perspective and adopting different strategies to intervene in the politics. But the fact remains that they are

45 Dr Sudha Ramachandran is an independent researcher and journalist based in Bangalore, India. She has written extensively on South Asian peace and conflict, political and security issues for *The Diplomat, Asia Times* and *Geopolitics*.

also political persons. To understand their politics, one has to see 'politics' itself in plural forms. As per Moser and Clark,

> ...a constant universal interpretation of agency across cultures cannot be assumed... 'Multiple realities' and the importance of place and location in the construction of identities and differences determine how identity and agency (knowledge/capability) are differently constituted. This, in turn, affects how actors attempt to cope with situations they face.
>
> (Moser and Clark, 2005, 5)

Women's politics, it needs to be noted, will be located in the context in which they are rooted. Hence, while being totally rooted in the patriarchal structures, women may be using varied strategies to respond, resist and even confront the power of the adversaries. At times, they may be using their very restricted gender space and role to negotiate for themselves as well as for men; and at other times they may be reinventing their roles to the process.

Women's Agency in Conflict Situation of Kashmir

In the conflict situation of Kashmir, women are essentially seen as victims. Much of the attention of the gender dimension of conflict there has been focused on women being the subject of rapes, killings and all kinds of human rights abuses. Attention has been also paid to the consequences women face due to the loss of their husbands. As widows and half widows, they are made to raise their children single-handedly with no economic support, to take care of the elderly at home, to head the household. They are shown to be grieving for their sons killed or missing in conflict. So, the whole discourse in Kashmir revolves around the victimhood of women. To quote Manchanda,

> The conservative patriarchal ideology of the Kashmir struggle casts women as symbols – grieving mother, martyr's mother and raped women. It developed an instrumental relationship with women as the frontline of the propaganda war over human rights violations by the Indian state and undervalued their activism, dismissing it as accidental.
>
> (Manchanda, 2001, 43)

There is no doubt that women have been impacted in the Kashmir conflict in the worst manner possible, but they have coped with the situation and ensured their survival during all kinds of situations in the last two and half decades. While the social structure of Kashmir, afflicted with patriarchy, does not allow them to be at the helm of affairs, they have placed their agency in the most innovative ways. However, the significance of the ways in which the women of Kashmir have displayed their agency has not been examined and analysed extensively.

Politicisation of Women

The post-1989 period was a time when there was sufficient politicisation of people. There was a very high level of politicisation across the class and gender divide, and women along with men became highly politicised. This was clearly reflected during our field study. Our respondents informed us that during this time, women along with men were intensely involved in the political questions of the time. Rabia (name changed), who is now a government official, stated,

> The period of early nineties was quite different. It was a period when everything seemed to have changed. I was a student in Aligarh. When I visited home during the winter of 1989-90, I could see the change. Everyone seemed to have become politicised. My friends and relatives were all discussing the political developments.... Even my politically disinterested female friends had become politicised. In the huge processions that we were witness to, almost on a daily basis, there was a strong presence of women.

Another respondent noted,

> There was overall increased interest and awareness among women about the political issues. Even not so literate women who would come to my house as domestic help would be discussing the political developments. Even the most ignorant were conscious that something was going on.

Since it was a time when there seemed to have been a strong wave of separatist response, people who were earlier not so politically active, were swayed by the momentum of things happening around. Ruby (name changed), who was a researcher in Kashmir University in the early nineties, noted that,

> There was an expectant air all around. Many of the male students whom we knew had gone underground. We knew about many of them having joined active militancy. A few of

> them would even visit the university once in a while, properly armed with guns. Among our friends, there would be open discussions as to what was happening.

The feeling, she says, was prevalent not only among the educated and politicised people but among every section of society.

The situation of militancy in post-1989 period was accompanied by a strong wave of separatism. Kashmiris on the whole were swayed by the separatist sentiment and reflected their identification with it by participating in the anti-state demonstrations that were taking place on a day-to-day basis. These processions included not only political and social activists but even ordinary citizens. Among those who participated in these processions were students, teachers, employees, housewives, workers, government employees and so on. These processions were being organised not only in Srinagar but in almost all the towns of Kashmir. Significantly, women were an important part of the demonstrations. Like men, they came out in large numbers to participate in processions. So large was their number and so much was their visibility that they became the face of the mass politics of separatism. Almost on a daily basis, there were mass protests, and women were at the forefront of these protests.

Kashmir has had a tradition of women participating in mass demonstrations. 'Outnumbering men at times, they would often make their presence felt in a big way in protest rallies and dangerous political missions (Krishna Misri, cited in Khan,

2009).' Though they were very much visible during the pre-1947 resistance politics, their presence in the protest politics in Kashmir during the 1953-1975 period was significantly noticeable. Their presence during the 1963 crisis following the theft of the holy relic in Kashmir has been recorded by many. The loss of the holy relic, believed to be the hair of Prophet Muhammad's moustache that is preserved in the Hazratbal shrine, created an emotional outburst in Kashmir. The massive protest demonstrations at that time had a large presence of women. The tradition of mass protests and participation of women in these protests continued even in later times. Women were on the streets in the 1976-77 period when there were massive protests against the withdrawal of support by the Congress Party to Sheikh Abdullah's government (formed in 1975 as a result of the Indira-Sheikh Accord). At this time, there was also a rumour about Sheikh Abdullah being severely indisposed. For days together, women from rural areas would march to the residence of Sheikh to show their solidarity with him. In 1977, when Sheikh Abdullah won the Assembly election with a massive mandate, women were there again on the streets celebrating the victory of JKNC. And when Sheikh died in 1982, they came out in huge numbers to mourn his death.

Throughout the later period also, women were quite visible in the public space. Hence, when protests started in Kashmir in the post-1987 period, women were an essential part of these. As the intensity of the protests increased, the number of women participants also increased. They would come from far-flung villages and join these marches held in Srinagar or other towns of Kashmir region. They would be sloganeering and marching long distances. What was peculiar about the participation of women in protest demonstrations during this period was that the class barrier that traditionally existed in such protests had been clearly transcended. Earlier, women who participated in protest demonstrations came from the lower income background, mostly from rural areas or from downtown areas of Srinagar. A large number of women belonging to the *Hanji* (boats people) community participated in street politics. The women from relatively better-off backgrounds, even from the lower middle class groups, would not be visible. With the norms of 'honour' being linked to the actions and identity of women in the Kashmiri middle class, they were discouraged from being seen in street politics. This was to change in the post-1987 period, particularly in the massive demonstrations of 1989-90. Women participating in these demonstrations would be from varying socio-economic backgrounds – educated, uneducated, from middle class and working class, professionals as well as ordinary women. It is a different matter that women from the elite and privileged classes still chose to stay away from the demonstrations.

In fact, the response of these classes to the situation, as it was unfolding, was quite different. Many of them shifted families and business to places outside Kashmir. While the rich class of exporters shifted to Delhi, Bombay or other big cities, the other privileged people like bureaucrats and highly placed professionals relocated their children for educational purposes to Delhi and other metropolitan cities. The outer areas of Srinagar city, called the Civil Lines, where the elite of Kashmir generally reside, remained mostly unaffected by the protest politics. As Rabia (name changed), who lives in posh Jawahar Nagar, related:

> The area was almost untouched by the processions, not only in 1989-90, but even in the later period. When things would be happening in Lal Chowk or Nowhatta, or there would be restriction of movement in these areas, life would be almost normal in these outer areas. Women of this area and other similar areas did not come out to demonstrate on the streets.

Tasneem (name changed), referring to the same distinction of localities and class distinction among people in Kashmir, said, 'If you really want to see women active in protest politics, come and see them in Maisuma, or in Dal Gate or in downtown areas.' This distinction of localities and class factor would be visible in later periods as well. Whether it was the mass demonstrations of 2008, 2010 or 2016, women from the downtown areas would be much more involved. They have actually been part of the stone throwing groups, playing ding dong battles with the security forces.

Women were not part of armed militancy in Kashmir. Though there have been reports of training camps for women militants established by LeT and even the arrest of a woman militant, there have not been many active women militants (Parashar, 2014, 87). As Parashar[46] notes, it was the conservative

46 Swati Parashar, a scholar of international acclaim has been working on Conflict and Gender issues.

nature of the politics and religious influence on the movement that women stayed away from militancy. As she notes,

> Groups like Harakat Ul-Mujahidin (HuM), the Harkat-ul-Jihad-al-Islami (HuJI), Jaish-e-Mohammed (JeM) and Lashkar-e-Taiba (LeT) have all been inspired by radical Islamist ideology in matters of gender, sexual division of labour and most importantly in their efforts to enlist the support of women. In what can be construed as a paradox, initially all those groups were opposed to involvement of women in the militancy. Jihad, outside the home, was considered strictly a male domination.
>
> (Parashar, 2014, 85)

So, on the whole, women did not pick up guns and join the cadre of militants. However, they played active roles in many other militancy-related activities. This was mainly due to the nature of the traditional society of Kashmir which though quite liberal and humanistic, draws a line between the roles of men and women. The influence of religion here is also very strong because of which women are not encouraged to play certain roles.

And yet, it cannot be stated that women had no association with militancy. Though the cadre of militants comprised mainly of men, and women did not participate in militant activities, yet they were the backbone of militancy, especially in the initial phase. On the whole, women were there as support to the militants and were ready to fill whatever role they were expected to in the situation. To quote Parashar, 'Women... were instrumental in acting as support groups for militant men.

They nursed and shielded the militants, and carried messages and arms (Parashar, 2011, 438).' They also played the most important role of legitimising the armed militancy.

This process of legitimisation involved a number of things ranging from eulogising the militants, giving them the status of public heroes to encouraging young boys, including their own children, to join the militancy. The militants who died were given the status of martyrs and women celebrated the funeral like wedding festivities. One can get an inkling of how women responded to armed militancy in the way they used the *wun wun* (the traditional marriage songs) to legitimise militancy. As Manisha Sobhrajani has noted in her translation of these marriage songs, the old songs were reformulated to incorporate the acts of the militants (Sobhrajani, 2008).[47]

In this way, women used their familial roles not only to legitimise the phenomenon of militancy but also to generate a general societal consent for the violence they were indulging in. As Parashar has noted,

> As mothers, they sang praises of the martyrdom of their sons, showered their dead bodies with dried fruits and inspired the men in their family to take up arms against the Indian state… and an aggressive and gun-wielding masculinity was embraced and legitimised by a society otherwise known for its pacifist and Sufi values.
>
> (Parashar, 2011, 438)

47 One can cite one of the wun wun songs as referred by Sobhrajani, *Kalashnikov lagai balayai, Yenav ladayat path fairaleh* (Don't give up this fight for freedom; I shower my life on this Kalashnikov) *Main mujahidov behan, Praraie hideoutas* (O my beloved mujahid, I will wait for you at the hideout) (Sobhrajani, 2008).

This was also clearly reflected during our field-study. Ruby, who is now in a teaching position, stated,

> During the early period of militancy, there was a lot of fascination for militancy and militants. Girls used to talk about militants, share stories about them and worship them as heroes. That was the time when there was a lot of idealism, and the people had not yet been disillusioned by armed militancy.

Shabnam (name changed), who was a college student during the early nineties, recalling those days, stated,

> We used to discuss militancy and share stories about our own brothers, cousins and boys in the neighbourhood. These stories fascinated us at that time. We used to take a lot of interest in them. Now things have changed. No more such hero-worship of militants takes place. But, at that time, it was a new phenomenon. So we all were curious to know more about the militants.

Militancy, it needs to be noted, in the initial years was intrinsically linked with the Kashmiri society. The first generation of militants were mostly local Kashmiris and therefore they were seen as heroes, and for that reason, militancy was seen as a strategy of resistance. Therefore, it had the approval of the society at large. However, by 1992-93, militancy had started losing its sheen. This was due to many reasons. For one, the earlier cadre of ideologically committed local youth was increasingly replaced by the foreign militants who were neither knowledgeable nor appreciative of the local culture. As compared to the ideologically oriented first generation of militants, many of whom were educated or dropouts from professional institutions, quite a few militants in the later period were lured by ulterior motives like money, status and power. They indulged in many activities which were opposed to the local sensitivities and this alienated the society from militancy. The capturing of Charar-e-Sharief, the shrine of Sheikh Noor-ud-din Noorani by Jihadis and its destruction during the encounter between the militants and the army was particularly responsible for turning Kashmiri women away from militancy in general, and Jihadi militants in particular. Sheikh Noor-ud-din Noorani is known to be the patron saint of Kashmir, and Charar-e-Sharief is known to be the most revered Sufi shrine.

However, the greater reason for the alienation of the society from militancy was the impact that violence had had on the society by then. The violence had so impacted the Kashmiri society that most people were trapped in the situation. In what became popularly known as 'the gun culture', there was no escape for the people. With increasing intensity of militancy and the militarisation of the Valley, people were constantly getting killed in the crossfire or were being abducted or had gone missing. This left an increasing number of widows or half-widows and orphans.

One reason for the Kashmiris' disenchantment with militants and militancy was their (militants') indulgence in criminal activities against the society in general and women in particular. These activities included extortion, forced marriages, sexual violence and other forced demands for food and shelter. Women particularly had to bear the major brunt of the situation. To quote Ramachandran and Jabbar, 'Hundreds of women are believed to have been raped by militants and security forces… Militants have raped women as a way of punishing other family members believed to be informers or suspected of opposing the militants (Ramachandran and Jabbar, 2003, 19).'[48] The armed militancy led to the militarisation of society and deeply impacted the social and cultural processes. With an overwhelming influence of 'gun-wielding' people and their intervention in cultural, religious and social matters and the assertion of masculinised discourse, women found space shrinking for them.

By mid-nineties, the shift in societal response towards militancy could be seen very clearly. The militants were no more celebrated as 'heroes' and were not welcomed at homes and streets the way they were in the earlier period of militancy. However, there continued to be exhibited a soft response towards the local militants. The death of a militant and the whole process of mourning reflected the response of women. A local militant was still seen as a 'martyr' and he got the respect of the society, even when there was an overall rejection of armed militancy. And yet, militancy as a phenomenon to

48 Sonia Jabbar is a writer, journalist, photographer, filmmaker and graphic designer who has been associated with various people's movements – feminist, anti-communal, sexual rights, anti-nuclear – and various initiatives on Pakistan-India peace and friendship. She has also worked in Kashmir as a human rights activist since 1995.

which Kashmiris related to in early nineties was de-legitimised, and women played an important role in it.

Role of Women in Conflict Politics in Post-1990 Period

The kind of visibility that women had in the early period of separatism and militancy in Kashmir was no more there in the post-1990 period. This was a phase of aggressive militancy and an equally aggressive response by the state. The kind of mass protests that were visible during the earlier phase were not held any more. In the overall context of extreme violence, political processes were fully grounded. In this situation of fear and insecurity, there was no space for public protest. Hence, in this phase, there was a withdrawal of women from the public space. As a respondent Naseema (name changed) noted,

> By mid-nineties, the situation in Kashmir had become very complex. It was not only the fear of harassment by the security forces but also the fear of militants and counter-militants. The glorification of militancy that was seen in early nineties was no more to be seen. In fact, there were many stories floating around about the kidnapping and forced marriages by the militants. By 1995-1996, we also became aware of the Ikhwanis. These were the surrendered militants who now worked for the security forces. They were the most feared ones because they enjoyed a lot of power. On the whole, we felt that we were surrounded by various types of guns – those of the security forces, of the militants and the counter-insurgents. We were literally living in a culture of violence.

However, women continued to play multiple roles in the conflict politics. As Ahmed[49] has noted, women played a role in negotiating for the men of the family. With the men in the family imprisoned, not-so-educated or even illiterate women would follow the legal suits; they came to be well-informed about the legal system thereby getting sufficient exposure in the process. 'Thus their personal tragedies made them emerge as empowered women, who control the lives of their kith and kin, despite the impediments of education, gender and birth (Ahmad, 2011).' As time passed, a large number of women had to substitute for men; they were forced to earn a livelihood and take up familial responsibilities. With large number of men missing or killed, it became their responsibility to provide for the needs of the children and educate them.

As the situation of conflict became more complex, the implications of the conflict for women also started becoming quite intricate. Women were now playing more complex roles. Anuradha Bhasin Jamwal notes that there was an 'increasing presence of women in the role of informers, couriers and sources – working both for the militants and the security forces' in the post-1996 period (Jamwal, 2010). She refers to the case of Shehnaz Kausar, who worked first for militants and then for the security forces, and notes how women like her became the victims of the situation.

49 Mushtaq Ul Haq Ahmad Sikander is writer-activist based in Srinagar, Kashmir.

Rita Manchanda also has noted the cases of women being enrolled by the state as informers. She refers to the case of Shahina who joined the CRPF as a constable. As per the statement of Shahina,

> Militant group Ikhwan ul Muslimeen had kidnapped her younger brother, hoping to recruit him. Desperate to secure his release, she went to the BSF camp. Her brother was rescued and two militants taken prisoner. Shahina then was kidnapped, first, by the JKLF and punished with 41 lashes, and later by Ikhwan militants who repeatedly raped her. Shahina escaped, and eventually joined the CRPF (Central Reserve Police Force) as a constable.
>
> (Manchanda, 1999)

Manchanda adds that there were some women who were part of the intelligence wings of security forces including CRPF and CID. But there were also a large number of widows and half widows who chose to be informers for money since they had lost earning male members.

Women and Conflict Politics in Post-2000 Period

Women started being visible once again in the public space in the post-militancy period. By 2004, the armed militancy had started declining, and in the new environment, the protest politics was again assuming importance. The year 2007 saw a number of protests in which women were as active as men. However, it was during the period of 2008-2010 that there was massive mobilisation of separatist space. In 2008, there was a prolonged agitation around the issue of diversion of state land to Shri Amarnathji Shrine Board. In 2009, there were frequent protests around the issue of alleged rape and killing of two women in Shopian, and in 2010, there was a massive upsurge around the issue of fake encounters that lasted the whole of summer months. During all these protests, there was massive mobilisation of people. Women were mobilised in large numbers and as always became the face of this mass politics. They also helped enforce the 'civil curfew'. Civil curfew was a separatist strategy which resulted in complete shutdown of business and trade, transport, educational institutions and other activities. Women, at this time, were also visible as stone pelters. As Aaliya Anjum notes in her article in *Al Jazeera*,

> In the mass protests of 2008 and 2010, an increasing number of women participated alongside men, at times even leading all-women protest marches.... These summer protests of 2008 and 2010 were punctuated by protesters pelting stones... Interestingly, women also engaged in stone throwing, together with chanting...slogans.
>
> (Anjum, 2011)

Women were similarly visible in the mass protest politics which took place a few years later in 2016. These protests that were held after the killing of Burhan Wani, the Hizbul Mujahideen militant, lasted for the whole of summer that year. Women at this time also were visible at the protest sites and were involved in stone pelting incidents.[50]

Separatist Leadership and Women

Despite the active association of women with the separatist politics in Kashmir, the separatist politics has been, more or less, dominated by men; women have been conspicuous by their absence in leadership positions. There have been few exceptions like Asiya Andrabi, who had some presence in this politics, but generally, not only the leadership but also the cadres of various separatist organisations have been manned by men only.

There appears to be a dividing line between the roles of men and women in the separatist politics – while women would be seen on the streets, in protest demonstrations and performing various ancillary roles, the organisational politics and leadership has been confined to men only. Hameeda Bano, an academician-cum-activist attributes this absence of women in leadership positions to the general political culture of Kashmir which is male oriented and does not have much space for women. Invisibility of women, according to her, is not a peculiarity of separatist politics but a reflection of the larger political scenario of Kashmir. Even in the mainstream

50 One incident which became very visible was that of college girls caught in cross-protests; these girls were also involved in stone pelting. This incident became so significant that the government took the decision of having a 500-women CRPF force to tackle the women stone pelters (Chauhan, 2018).
Decision was later taken that 'Around 1,000 women will be hired in Jammu and Kashmir for a police battalion, which will primarily deal with incidents like stone pelting in the Valley (*Economic Times*, 2018).'

politics, there are not many women, and those who are there are not because they are capable leaders, but because of their family connections. Citing the example of the two Kashmiri women leaders in mainstream politics – Mehbooba Mufti and Sakina Ittoo, Hameeda Bano refers to their family background (Hameeda Bano, quoted in DasGupta, 2001, 30). In both cases, these women found it convenient to join politics because their fathers were active in politics.

Women's space in separatist politics is therefore a reflection of the political environment of Kashmir, which is generally not very congenial for women. Despite being educated and pursuing careers, women here are essentially seen as home makers. Political roles which fall within the confines of public roles are therefore not very easily accessible for them, unless there is familial support. With the exception of certain 'political families' which provide such a support to their women, women are generally not encouraged to be visible in the public space. And in extraordinary circumstances like the conflict situation, when women attain visibility, this is mainly in relation to roles which can be seen as an extension of familial roles. So, in reality, it is roles like 'motherhood' that get celebrated in conflict politics.

One of the categories in which women in conflict situation have attained visibility in Kashmir is the category of 'widows' or 'half-widows'. This again is a reflection of their status not as individuals but in relation to men in the family.

The domestic space arguably is the 'private' space where women are supposedly 'protected' and 'secure' and therefore even when they enter the 'public space' it is only for the specific purpose of getting educated or for the purpose of working or pursuing their careers. Beyond this purpose, the public space is not considered 'proper' for women and in the general social understanding carries all the possibilities of not only endangering the 'security and safety' of women but also upsetting the social and ethical order.

This traditional definition of essential women has widespread acceptance not only among men but also among women. There have been radical leaders like Asiya Andrabi of Dukhtaran-e-Millat (DeM) – an all-women organisation, who believe in the demarcation of roles of men and women in the politics of Kashmir. For Andrabi, the gender division of roles – with men being active in public space and women being confined to domestic space – is very logical. She not only wants women to be confined to the home, but also be veiled all the time.[51]

The gender hierarchy that operates in the social sphere also gets reflected in the political sphere as much in mainstream politics as in separatist politics. To quote Manchanda, 'Fear of social censure in a deeply conservative society has inhibited the organised activism of women and prevented many from assuming political roles (Manchanda, 2011).

51 On being questioned as to why women were not in leadership positions, many of our respondents also stated that they did not find anything wrong with that. Since women were involved in the significant job of taking care of the family, they could not be expected to be militants or separatist leaders. Who would take care of the family, who would cook and who would do the daily chores – if both men and women became combatants? they asked.

In the male-dominated and traditional society of Kashmir, women are not supposed to be competing with men and playing an equal role in politics. That is the reason some militant and separatist organisations, despite having a women's wing, did not develop women's leadership. The JKLF was the first separatist/militant organisation to have a women's branch called Muslim Khawateen Markaz (MKM) which was led by Madam Bakhtawar. When Hurriyat Conference was organised, the MKM became a part of the Hurriyat. Similarly, the Hizbul Mujahideen had a women's wing called Binat-ul-Islam. Most of these organisations were delinked from political activities and were known to be involved only in humanitarian activities. These organisations were mostly manned by the relatives of male militants and provided ancillary services to the militants – like carrying messages or arms, visiting the houses of slain militants and supporting their families. It is for this reason that the small number of women in the separatist political space, who have made some name for themselves, are not treated at par with the male leaders. Zamrooda Habib, whose organisation MKM is part of the Hurriyat Conference, has noted a gender divide within separatist politics. In her opinion, women separatist leaders find it quite difficult to get an acknowledgement of their role by the male-dominated group of separatists. They are neither given an equal space with the male leaders nor seen as 'leaders in their own right'. In fact, Zamrooda has noted her disappointment with the separatist leadership in her memoir *Qaidi No. 100*. Though her all-women's organisation has been a part of the Hurriyat Conference right from the beginning, she felt neglected within the separatist politics. After she was arrested, she was left to fend for herself. As Manchanda notes, 'The Hurriyat disowned her.'

Women's Agency and Silent Resistance

In understanding women's agency in Kashmir conflict, one has to focus on their silent resistance against the forces that sought to push them further to the margins. As one can assess, three decades after the militancy started, women have emerged as survivors in the context of onslaught on their rights – be those related to their freedom, their right to movement, right to education and the like. This onslaught was really serious, particularly during the peak of militancy.

Early 1990s was the period when all kinds of political forces were unleashed in Kashmir. This was the time when there was mushrooming of militant organisations. Besides the local organisations, there were many foreign-based Jihadi organisations. Of these organisations, there were those which were ideologically fundamentalist. Apart from being involved in the militant activities, they were also enforcing cultural and religious norms. Most of these norms were oriented towards women and sought not only to push them away from the public space but also to subject them to a restricted life. Thus, dress codes were imposed and women were asked to veil themselves. Western dresses were declared taboo. Efforts were also made to impose sex-segregation in public spaces and campaign was launched against co-education. While sources of public entertainment like cinemas and video-parlours were banned, beauty parlours were also banned. There were many other practices which were declared un-Islamic and were banned. Use of contraceptives and abortion were among such practices.

There are many stories of the early militancy period when all kinds of dictates were issued. As reported by Women's Initiative, in early nineties, schools were pressurised to change uniforms of girls. As 'an over-reaction to felt cultural imperialism', some militants imposed restrictions on girls wearing skirts and jeans. A missionary school withstood the pressure for some time, but finally gave in and changed the uniform from skirts to *salwar kameez* (Dewan, 1994, 2656).

Citing another situation, Ramachandran and Jabbar have noted, 'The sale of contraceptives was stopped and family planning procedures were not performed, at least openly in the hospitals.' The practices related to family planning were not only seen as un-Islamic but also as against the requirement of Kashmiri society. Organisations like Jamaat-e-Islami and Banat-ul-Islam asked people not to kill unborn children. 'People especially in the villages were told that the Central government was trying to alter the Muslim Majority nature of the State and so Muslims should have more children. Besides, the armed struggle needed more fighters (Ramachandran and Jabbar, 2003, 21).' There were stories about women facing acid attacks for not adhering to the commands of the militants.

In such a situation, where certain fringe organisations were seeking to impose norms that were alien to Kashmiri society, there was no resistance from the political class or the society. While the mainstream politics had collapsed and political leaders had withdrawn from the public space, no opposition was offered by the separatist organisations. Even the militant organisations, which otherwise claimed to be rejecting the role of religion in politics, had no objections to the dictates issued by these organisations.

Since the writ of the militant organisations was the most powerful one, women had not many choices. They were compelled to follow any command.

Of the many campaigns that were launched by the fringe organisations, one was related to veiling women. Women were asked to wear the *burqa* (veil) or at least adopt the *hijab* (head scarf). Off and on, one or the other militant organisation would issue a threat to women asking them to veil themselves or face the consequences. It is interesting to note the response of Kashmiri women to this campaign.

Whenever a command was issued, women would follow it but wait for the pressure to be eased and then get back to their normal dressing. They would not make the veil a part of their routine dress.[52] Their general approach to the issue gets reflected in the response of Farhat, a Srinagar-based housewife who completed her postgraduate education in the 1970s:

> We were not used to burqa. In my neighbourhood, women did not use burqa at all. Even in my college days and

---

52 Since full veil or burqa has never been a part of the dress code of Kashmiri women, they did not feel very comfortable around it. There were two classes of women who adored the burqa – either the very elite women who wanted to flaunt their distinctive status or few rural women. In this second case, the burqa that was used was not the black burqa but a peculiar type of white burqa.

> University days, there were no women in our circle wearing burqa. Rarely, on the roadside, we would find women with black burqa. Compared to the black burqa, we were more used to the white burqa which was adopted by few women of rural background.

Militancy however changed things. To quote her,

> Things certainly became different after the onset of militancy. A number of times, there were calls from the militants that women be veiled. Each time the call came, we were advised by the family to adhere to the call for the sake of our safety. We used to hear all sorts of stories of girls being penalised and acid being thrown on their faces. So we had no option but to adopt the burqa. I remember the first time I had to wear a burqa; I felt very much uncomfortable and physically restrained. Later on, we became more practical about the issue because we knew that the call of veiling women would not last for long, and that we have to compromise for the time being.

Not having any expectation of support from the civil society or the political leadership, most of the women adopted a pragmatic approach to the question of veiling. Rabia who is now a government official, thus stated,

> We were young and saw things from a different perspective. Although I did not wear burqa generally, but during the periods when it became compulsory to wear a burqa, I would watch my friends to see what kind of cloth and texture they were buying. We would look for fashionable burqas, with lot

> of imported laces and very delicate embroidery. I remember a friend of mine who recommended us to a tailor who made beautiful *Abhayas.*

As this statement shows, women's response to the issue of veiling was quite strategic – wearing it when forced to, but rather than fulfilling the objective of the militants to push women to the margins and make them obscure, they also used it as a fashion symbol. They made it attractive and fashionable. This was more clearly so for the hijab or the head scarf that they were expected to wear. In the early 1990s, young militants or militant supporters would take upon themselves the role of keeping a vigil on women – checking the public transports to see if women were 'appropriately' dressed.

For most women, use of Hijab was a convenient way to negotiate their space in public places. As Ruby, a non-Muslim teacher, thus reminisced:

> During the early period of militancy, even I used to carry a scarf in my bag. I did not want to be isolated and seen as different from other women. Once, when we were coming back from our work place, our bus got stuck due to a procession. We were asked to get down from the bus. Immediately, I took out the scarf and covered my head with it. I felt quite safe after that.

She explained that this pressure to conform to the expectation of the dominant political actors – the militants – was felt by most of the women. And rather than willingly accept the veil or scarf, they did it in strategic ways, to protect themselves.

However, there were women who adopted the scarf for religious and political reasons. As explained by Nahid (name changed),

> Since the beginning of militancy, women, like men in Kashmir, have become conscious of their Muslim identity. Rather than looking towards the Indian sub-continent, they have started looking towards countries like Iran and the Arab countries for their inspiration. That is the reason why most of the Abhayas in vogue are not Kashmiri in origin but are of Iranian type.

This statement reflects a part of Kashmiri reality. One can find a definite change in the dressing style of women. The number of women who have adopted the veil might be quite low, but the number of women who have adopted the scarf has certainly increased. Shazia, a homemaker, stated that the use of scarves is not merely due to the pressure of militants. Some women adopted it even when no such call was given by the militants. She cited the examples of her own daughters.

> I have two daughters of almost the same age, with one year of difference. My elder daughter is just like me. She is very fashionable and keeps up with the latest styles. She likes to wear jeans and does not like to cover her head. But my younger daughter, since last couple of years, has adopted the scarf and is very rigid about it. I feel that it is the influence of school, friends and the media.

Similar responses were given by a couple of other respondents. To cite a few examples:

> I do not see any reason why the whole issue of women using hijab or scarf should be debated. It is my identity; I wear it because I am a Muslim and I see nothing wrong in that. Why does no one question what other people wear? Why do the western girls wear skirt or why do Hindu women use the *bindi*?

> I am very happy that I have adopted the scarf. I feel more rooted as a Muslim. Earlier, I would be just a part of the crowd and no one would be able to distinguish as to who I am. But now everyone can see that I am a Muslim, a practicing Muslim. It is not that I have made only cosmetic changes in myself. I have become religious in the real sense of the term. I pray five times; I fast throughout the month of Ramzan and I am trying to be a pious Muslim in my behaviour.

However, while the scarf has been more willingly adopted by Kashmiri women, there has been resistance to making burqa a part of their normal attire. Though there has certainly been an increase in the number of women using burqa, yet it has not become a dress widely used. This despite the fact that throughout the period of militancy, the call for fully veiling women was given quite frequently. On the whole, women have consciously rejected it and silently but very forcefully resisted it. But this is not just about the burqa, women have silently resisted various other kinds of pressures upon them. In early nineties, attempts were also made to introduce the idea of sex-segregation in public places, for instance in the buses. Also, there were efforts to oppose the idea of co-education.[53]

Though affected due to the prolonged period of the abnormal situation, education of women has remained a priority for the Kashmiri society. Although there has always been a lag between males and females, yet the number of educated women has increased tremendously since 1947. What is more important is that the society values the education of women and does not place any restriction on women's mobility or their being educated in co-educational institutions.

The vibrant educational sector of Kashmir specifically provides a very impressive picture of women as survivors. They have shown their resilience throughout the period of conflict. The number of girls in all educational institutions is increasing and even in the co-educational institutions, there is a large number of girls. The universities of Kashmir provide a very clear reflection of the interest taken by women not only in conventional fields of education but also in the new scientific, technical and management-related fields. Women are competing for professional courses and opting for technical lines not only nearer home but in Jammu and various parts of the country. As per a respondent, 'Career consciousness among women has increased. They are competitive and are planning

53 According to Ramachandran and Jabbar '...women have resisted the restrictions imposed on them.... They have, for instance, refused to wear the burqa, which they say is not a part of Kashmiri tradition, although they do cover their heads with a scarf. They have circumvented the ban on abortions and use of family planning procedures by going to Jammu for the same or having them done in Srinagar after paying a hefty sum. But these are individual efforts (Ramachandran and Jabbar, 2003, 23-24).'

their careers from the time they are in high school.' Emaan, a middle-aged respondent stated,

> The times have changed so much. When we were young, there were not many career options available for us. The most popular choice was either to be a doctor or a teacher. But now there are so many career options for girls. In any case, there is no difference between girls and boys so far as these choices are concerned. In fact, I find girls pursuing their education as well as their career choices very aggressively. They are doing better than boys and are keen to try new lines. I am really surprised by the level of information the younger generation of girls have about the technical lines available for them.

Women, therefore, have been able to preserve their visibility in the public spaces. Militancy certainly posed problems for them, especially during the period of intense violence. Besides the fear of being caught in the crossfire between the security forces and the militants, there was the fear of being sexually abused. Hence, the mobility of women during the peak of militancy was restricted. However, that has not become a permanent feature of life in Kashmir. Women are as much mobile on the streets now and are found to be taking all kinds of jobs and pursuing all modern career options. This is not to say that women are at par with men, that they don't face discrimination. In the given situation of patriarchy, they are certainly discriminated against. But as they avail the education and career opportunities, it shows they have clearly moved ahead during the period of militancy. There is certainly a larger number of women who are being trained as doctors and engineers, who are pursuing MBA, opting for more challenging options like information technology, etcetera.

On the whole, one agrees with DasGupta that,

> Even amidst this atmosphere of violence and terror, the women of Kashmir have shown resistance and a sense of discrimination. They have refused to give up their traditional value system and cherished heritage. Had they not resisted the pressures to succumb to social customs that were alien to the Kashmiri way of life, perhaps Kashmir would have gone the way of Afghanistan.
>
> (DasGupta, 2001, 20)

The fear of the traditional culture of Kashmiri society being altered was always alive. However, it was mainly due to the determined though silent resistance of women that this fear did not assume the shape of reality. Women, while identifying with the separatist politics during its peak, saw to it that they were not adversely affected by the campaigns of the reactionary forces. The nature of resistance was certainly at the individual level. There was no organised resistance, not even a campaign. It was therefore at the individual level that the women used their agency and offered their resistance.

That women have come this far, is really commendable, given the fact that the situation has generally been difficult for women, especially during the peak of militancy This becomes clear from the following response of Razia (name changed), a researcher in the University of Kashmir. She thus notes:

It was difficult growing up during the early period of militancy. Throughout our schooling, we were faced with so many problems. The process of education was discontinuous. During my early childhood, there were long breaks. Schools were not functional for days and months together. Our parents would cover the school curriculum at home since the same could not be completed at school. During these breaks, I used to feel suffocated sitting at home and longed to go to school and meet friends. We could not move around freely in the city as well, since there was no normal life in the city. As I grew up, I faced other problems while traveling outside the house. There were times when we were stuck in situations which generated a lot of fear among us. While in school, sometimes we would be detained even after the school hours because there was a bomb explosion or crossfire nearby. While traveling back from school, we would be really scared. However, once we went to college, the situation changed somewhat. But what affected us most was the uncertainty of things. At times, life seemed to be absolutely normal; bazaars would be full of people, shops would be full of beautiful things, and even occasional festivities would be there. Then all of a sudden, something would happen, and life on the streets would come to a standstill. However, we got used to this change of moods on the streets also, and when I look back, I feel very surprised that I have come this far. I have had so many gaps, discontinuities in my education, and yet I feel capable of taking up any kind of challenge.

Similar experiences of getting educated in the violence-ridden Valley has been narrated by many women. As Salma (name changed), a respondent from Srinagar, narrated,

> My family was not conservative and did not put any restriction on my education. But there were times when I felt really constrained by the situation. I remember once while coming back from college, my friend and I were walking along the footpath on the Residency Road when suddenly there was an explosion. Everyone ran here and there. We immediately rushed into a shop. The shopkeeper downed the shutter and we were there for a long time. When we came out, we realised that had we not rushed inside the shop, we could have been among the injured and dead who were lying in a pool of blood outside. I was really shaken with this encounter and I kept on thinking, it could be us, it could be us!

However, despite these experiences, women have shown their resilience and rather than merely surviving as victims of violence, they have come out as stronger and more confident women. They have coped and are part of a vibrant society.

The situation was much more tough for women in the remote and rural areas. Educating girls in the overall context of violence and militarisation had its own challenges. Nusrat (name changed) thus told her story of fighting the odds and reaching up to the University level. The fact that she was able to reach that level, and succeeded not only in finishing her Master's degree but also joining a research group, was a great achievement, and she attributes it all to the 'grace of God'. To quote her:

It was quite a struggle growing up during the period of militancy. There was every possibility that I could not have completed my studies. But it was only by the will of God that I could cross all the barriers – and to tell you the truth there were many barriers. There were times when we were advised to stay at home. It could be any situation – the security forces would be searching for a militant after an attack on them; or there would be a call for *hartal*; or there would be news of the death of a militant belonging to the village – anything could trigger a tension in the village and we would be made to sit at home. As I grew up, we had to cross a road which touched an army camp. Our parents would be very anxious. My grandmother often asked my father to stop my schooling since there was so much uncertainty on the streets. Luckily, my father did not pay heed to my grandmother. Schooling was still better; it became worse when we reached college. I had to travel around ten kilometres to reach my college and the pressure of my grandmother had started increasing. Even my mother at times would feel very uncomfortable and she would join my grandmother in pleading with my father to stop my education. Once we were stuck in the bus because the road was closed due to an encounter taking place. That day, both, my mother and grandmother, were belligerent and said that enough was enough and there would be no more college for me. For a week or so, I was forced to sit at home. But then my father intervened and accompanied me to college for a number of days. It was really a touch-and-go situation. My education is God's grace upon me, otherwise, the situation did not allow it.

Women and Agitational Politics

While Kashmir has been known for its politics of resistance and protests, Jammu has had a history of agitational politics. Right from the early 1950s, there have been major agitations in the region. These agitations have been mostly linked to the perceptions about the regional imbalances within the state of J&K and the consequent discrimination and neglect of the Jammu region. The year 1947 marked a major shift in the power structure of the state. Power was shifted from the Dogra monarch to the National Conference. Since National Conference has mainly been a Kashmir-based party, having not only its mass base in the Valley, but its leadership also mostly coming from that region, there has been a perception that the Jammu region has been neglected politically. This perception continued throughout the later period. Even when the JKNC merged with the Congress Party in 1965, the perceptions remained the same as the political elite structure continued to be dominated by the Kashmiri leaders. With Jammu lacking a regional party at par with JKNC and lacking the kind of leadership Kashmir had, this region suffered from a political void and invisibility. This lack of political parity with the Kashmir region was recognised by the Gajendragadkar Commission Report. It made some recommendations related to re-structuring the power politics, particularly those related to greater visibility of the Jammu region within the government. However, the recommendations of this Commission notwithstanding, the regional discontent continued. Throughout the 1970s and 1980s, the regional identity politics revolved around the political neglect and political deprivation of Jammu region.

Despite the fact that the nature of power politics changed in the post-2002 period and Jammu region got a share in power politics through the system of coalitions, yet the political discontent continued. All the coalitions that were formed during this period were based on an alliance between a Kashmir-based party and a Jammu-based party – Congress and PDP in 2002-2008; Congress and JKNC in 2009-2014 and; BJP and PDP in 2014-2018.

However, even during this period, there remained a deep-rooted perception in Jammu that the region faced political neglect and deprivation.

It is in this context of perpetuated perceptions about Jammu's neglect that there has been a wide-ranging discontent in the region. This discontent has often manifested in the regional agitations that have erupted from time to time.

The agitational response of Jammu is reflected in the various agitations in the region – while in 1952 there was a prolonged agitation known as the Praja Parishad agitation, in 2008, there was a similarly prolonged agitation called the Amarnath agitation. Between these two agitations, there have been numerous smaller or bigger agitations that have marked the politics of the region.

What has been the role of women in these agitations? It is an intriguing question and the answer to it would reflect the nature of women's participation in the non-electoral politics of Jammu region.

Praja Parishad and Other Agitations in Jammu Region

As stated above, the Praja Parishad agitation was a prolonged one and reflected Jammu's discontent vis-à-vis the changes that had taken place not only in the political structure of the state but also in the economy of the region. Soon after the JKNC took over power, it initiated major land reforms that were aimed at dismantling the feudal structures. Since the JKNC did not have much presence in Jammu region, these reforms and other economic policies did not take into consideration the regional sensibilities. Therefore, apart from the privileged landed classes, it also affected the interests of the middle-class residents of Jammu region.

The land reform laws passed by the National Conference in the 1948-1950 period have been hailed as very progressive since these were aimed at targeting the concentration of land in few hands and ameliorating the conditions of the oppressed landless peasantry. Apart from abolishing the class of intermediaries, these reform laws imposed ceiling on the landholding. The surplus land acquired by the state was redistributed among the landless peasants.

The ceiling laws affected a large landholding class in Jammu region – much more so because there was no provision for compensation at par with land acquisition provision in the rest of India. This class that was closely affiliated with the Dogra ruler was quite discontented with the shift in power.

However, the discontent in Jammu region in the post-1947 period was not restricted to the dispossession of the privileged classes. There were other reasons for the discontent. The political and economic changes that were taking place under the JKNC government were mainly in continuity with the identity politics of Kashmir region, and did not reflect the political sensibilities of Jammu region. Unlike Kashmir region, there was a different economic structure in Jammu region with most of the people dependent on trade, small businesses and entry into armed forces. But due to the policies followed by the JKNC, all these avenues were affected. Even though there was a class of landless peasants, mostly Dalits, who were benefited by the land redistribution policy of JKNC, large number of small traders were affected by the policy of state monopoly and control. The other source of employment – entry into the State's Armed forces – was severely impacted as the Dogra force was disbanded. Meanwhile, the small and middle class of landholders also had grievances due to the uniform application of ceiling laws for the fertile land of Kashmir and infertile land of Jammu. Since much of the land in Jammu was infertile and did not yield as much harvest, the equal ceiling law was affecting the not-so-rich land owners.

While the shift in power from the Dogra monarch to the National Conference resulted in a sense of satisfaction in Kashmir region, in Jammu there was a deep-rooted discontent. Apart from the fact that there was an adverse impact of the new policies being followed by the JKNC government, there were psychological and political reasons for this discontent. Psychologically, the shift was seen in regional terms. There was no anti-feudal movement in Jammu region and the Dogras of Jammu identified with the ruler; hence the abdication of power by the Dogra ruler was seen as a shift of power from the Jammu region to Kashmir.

More importantly, there was a political reason for the discontent. This was because the National Conference had no presence in Jammu region and hence did not extend its politics to the region. Therefore, there was neither a sense of identification with this party nor with the government. On the contrary, the party was seen to be specifically oriented towards the Kashmir region, pursuing the interest of Kashmiri people. There was no JKNC leader with a base in Jammu who could act as a bridge and link the people of Jammu with the government and its policies.

It is in this context that one must visualise the widely prevalent discontent in Jammu region in the post-1947 period. This disconnect was articulated by the Praja Parishad, a local party that was established after the accession of the state to India with the backing of the Bharatiya Jana Sangh and other Hindu Rightist organisations. 'Though its major support base comprised the disgruntled classes including the big and the medium landowners, the officials employed by the Maharaja in various bureaucratic positions, the large trading class, the ex-army officials; it came to be supported by many others who perceived the policies of the National Conference as biased against Jammu (Chowdhary, 2016).' The Parishad linked the discontent of the people with the ideological opposition of the Hindu Rightist parties against the Article 370 and launched a massive agitation against the Article. The agitation that was launched in 1952 raised the slogan of *ek Vidhan, ek Pradhan, ek Nishan.* It demanded complete constitutional integration of the state with India.

The Praja Parishad agitation, for all practical purposes, was a widespread agitation that involved the urban people, not only in Jammu city but in other towns of Jammu region with a predominantly Hindu population – like Kathua, Samba, Udhampur, Reasi etcetera. Since there has been no record of women's participation per se, we cannot specifically comment on the role of women in that agitation. However, the analysis of the leadership of the movement clearly reflects that it was mainly an agitation led by male leaders and the women did not have any significant presence in the leadership positions. However, the movement did have the support of women as the politics of the region at that point of time (as at any other moment) was based on the family as a unit.

The Praja Parishad agitation was significant from the perspective that it generated a political common sense among the urban population of the region related to Jammu's discrimination vis-à-vis Kashmir and its opposition to Article 370. This political common sense was as strongly shared by women as by men.

Agitational politics continued to be the essence of Jammu's vocal politics for the next few decades. Since the Jammu-based parties and political class was not significantly represented in power politics, the method of agitation was followed to assert Jammu's regional identity and its political discontent.[54]

Among the major agitations that took place in Jammu region was a students' agitation in 1966. The agitation was started over the issue of establishment of educational institutions in Jammu region. With a deep-seated feeling that the state government was discriminating against the region and not providing proper educational infrastructure in Jammu region – including universities, technical and professional institutions, etcetera – this agitation was started around the demand for establishment of an Ayurvedic College. The agitation, though started in Jammu city, spread beyond it. In a confrontation with the police, four students lost their lives. So massive was the agitation that the Central Government had to intervene, and a Commission of Inquiry, namely, the

---

54 This was mainly due to a perception that the power politics of the state did not represent the Jammu region and Jammu's discontent was mainly reflected in the agitational politics. How the agitational politics represented the political psyche of Jammu region was clearly reflected in a political ritual that was annually observed in the region – this was a call for protest on the first day of opening of government offices in Jammu as part of the 'Darbar Move' to the city of Jammu during the winter months. Invariable a call was given for Jammu Bandh on this day and the major opposition parties would demonstrate before the State Secretariat.

Gajendragadkar Commission of Inquiry was appointed to look into the grievances of Jammu region.

Similarly, in 1978, another agitation started in Poonch town, but soon took the form of a regional agitation. This agitation revolved around the issue of employment of Jammu youth in state jobs. The agitation was quite massive and lasted for a few months. The major focus of the agitation was on the alleged discriminatory practices of the state government towards Jammu region in the matter of state employment. This agitation was also followed by a Commission of Inquiry – the Sikri Commission.

Among the other agitations that took place in the subsequent years included the agitation against the state government's move to stop the movement of Darbar (state government) to Jammu region in 1987; the 1988 Reasi agitation with the demand for carving Reasi as a separate district; AIIMS agitation in 2015 demanding the location of AIIMS in Jammu region (and not in Kashmir).

Though all these agitations remained more or less concentrated in the heart of the cities, which invariably were urban, roping in the somewhat educated segments of society, they did assume a mass character due to the overwhelming participation of the people of the region.

Any protest which assumes a mass character invariably involves presence of women, but, if we go to the available records, there does not exist any reference to their contribution. Since educational institutions remained the most active space for mobilising the youth, one can assume that women and girl students would have been part of the agitating students. While collecting information about some of the agitations, we learned that whenever such regional agitations took place and students were mobilised, women students were very much part of the protesting mass. Rajni (name changed), a retired teacher, who was a post-graduate student during the 1978 agitation, reminiscing about the agitation stated:

> I remember that agitation very well. Our classes were disrupted for a long time and there were a lot of disturbances. We were attending class one day when suddenly the door was opened and a number of male students entered. They gave us a brief information about the agitation and asked us all to boycott the classes. Immediately we all came out of the class. We formed a sort of procession and walked up to the Canal Road repeating the slogans that were being raised.

On being asked whether women played any distinctive role in the agitation, she thus stated:

> I don't remember women playing any leadership role. The marches that we participated in were all led by male students. Not all the girls participated. Most of them just went home, even when the boys kept on pleading with us to join. But there were few of us who joined the march. I joined the students march a number of times. No one in my family minded it. My brother who was younger than me and was studying in one of the boys' colleges was also participating in the agitation and so were my uncles who were shopkeepers. My father being a government servant did not participate in the agitation, but

> he did not mind me being part of it. In family discussions, everyone agreed on the importance of assertion of the regional identity of Jammu. The region has been discriminated against and we need to raise our voices, we were told.

Despite the fact that the 1978 agitation was mainly led by males, there is some reference to the role played by women. In a function to promote leadership amongst women, conducted by the women's wing of Panthers Party, the General Secretary of the Party, Anita Thakur, recalled how women kept the Poonch agitation alive in 1978 after the arrest of all male leaders; they faced numerous actions to stop them by the police and administration but never gave up the fight (*Cross Town News*, 2019).

Women form a significant part of any commemoration or celebration held in honour of all these agitations. For example, every year three days are informally commemorated all over Jammu as 'Black Days'. These 'Black Days' are observed in memory of the students who laid down their lives in the 1966 agitation; male and female students all over Jammu region participate in the various students' activities. Woman students participate equally in all the events.

Amarnath Agitation

The Amarnath agitation was one such agitation which shook the whole of Jammu and Kashmir. To begin with, this agitation started in Kashmir against a government order which transferred forest land to the Shri Amarnathji Shrine Board (SASB) for constructing temporary facilities for the Amarnath pilgrimages taking place during two summer months every year. The land transfer order was opposed in Kashmir region by almost all political organisations – not only the separatist parties but also by the mainstream parties. PDP, which by itself was a part of the ruling coalition and was responsible for taking the decision of transfer of forest land to the SASB, started protesting against the decision. The order was projected as part of a larger conspiracy of the state to change the demography of Jammu and Kashmir. Such was the belief in this conspiracy theory that there was a massive upsurge which took a separatist turn. The separatist leadership mobilised the Kashmiris to such an extent that there were huge demonstrations on a daily basis. To mobilise and organise the agitations on a day-to-day basis, the Action Committee Against Land Transfer (ACALT) was formed. It was the sheer pervasiveness of aggressive Kashmiri response that led not only to the collapse of the state government but also withdrawal of the order.

The withdrawal of the land transfer order, however, resulted in a counter-agitation in Jammu region. This withdrawal was seen as hurting religious sentiments of Hindus. Soon the agitation became widespread with Hindu rightist parties and organisations coming openly in its support. The agitation that lasted for more than two months spread to almost all parts of Jammu region with people from different cross-sections of society supporting it. Though the core point of the agitation was religious, it also assumed a regional nature. The withdrawal of the land transfer order was linked with the regional discrimination and neglect. After the 1952 Praja

Parishad agitation, this was one of the most massive, popular and participatory agitations.

What made it a truly participatory agitation was the very visible role of women in it. Women not only emerged as the most crucial participants of the agitation, giving it a mass character, but were also seen as the central characters of the agitation.

To understand the nature of women's participation in this agitation, one needs to describe the various modes of protest that were followed in it. Since the agitation lasted for more than two months, different methods of political mobilisations as well as political actions were followed that helped in sustaining it for such a long time. The most significant method of representing the agitational mood of the region was the call for *bandh* or shutdown. What it involved was the suspension of all business and commercial activities as well as other public activities, most importantly the shutdown of shops, trading and educational institutions, transport, etcetera. Even the government offices were not allowed to be opened. The call for shutdown was given right at the beginning of the agitation, and it kept on being extended. The social and political activists meanwhile kept up the tempo by holding regular protest meetings in prominent places, and often courting jail for violating the government restrictions on meetings. Further, for involving the people of the region, various other activities were organised. These included processions in different parts of the region. These processions presented very visible signs of ongoing protests, and the participation of people in large numbers reflected how the agitation was taking deeper roots in the society. Among other methods, one most visible method was blocking of the highway, especially the Jammu-Kashmir Highways linking Jammu region with Punjab and Kashmir. Blocking of major bridges within the Jammu city was also frequently resorted to.

Since the 'hurt religious sentiment' was one of the major reasons for the agitation, there was lot of religious mobilisation to reflect the support of the people for the agitation. Religious gatherings like *kirtans* (chanting), *Prabhat Feris*[55] and various other religious activities were therefore organised almost on a daily basis. Most of these activities were systematically organised under the auspices of Shri Amarnath Yatra Sangharsh Samiti (SAYSS).

The agitation was quite widespread and involved almost all sections of society. Though mainly religious in nature, it was also seen as an agitation for regional assertion. This political nature of the agitation gave it more vibrancy, and different regional organisations started pledging their support for the agitation. Thus Jammu Chamber of Commerce, Jammu Bar, various teachers' associations including Jammu University Teachers' Association, organisations representing journalists, traders, and people of various other professions came out openly in support of the agitation. To show their identification with the agitation, people used various methods. The lawyers

55 *Prabhat Feri* is a traditional religious activity where people come out in a group in the morning singing religious songs.

for instance had a sit-out outside the High Court complex. Signature campaigns were organised at various places.

Initially the agitation had only high visibility of men; like in all the agitations, mainly men participated. However, later women also started attaining visibility as they began participating in the rallies and other activities. However, even when women participated, there were certain activities which remained male-oriented – street protests with activities like burning of tyres, burning of effigies; smashing windows of buses or damaging of public property; damaging electric meters; disrupting vehicular movement; ding-dong battles with police, and so on were mostly male activities. At some point of time, the chain hunger strikes were started and this was also an all-male affair. The addressing of public rallies was also mostly a male affair; though some women were seen addressing people, their presence was quite disproportionately small compared to their presence in the agitation. Similarly, the decision making within the Sangharsh Samiti was also a male affair. SAYSS had no female members. There was not much visibility of women in this organisation. And when decisions were announced and press conferences were held, it was exclusively a sphere of men.

But as stated above, as the agitation progressed, women's presence in the agitation became quite notable. Their numbers in the rallies started increasing and soon there were exclusively women's activities that attracted the attention of the people. For instance, there were women's *Prabhat Feris*. Women would also participate in processions and rallies which were either exclusively women's affairs or women joining men in such activities.

When women started joining rallies, a religious fervour was created; they sang *bhajans*, performed *kirtans,* and shouted *bham bham bhole* slogans. Religious processions were organised on an every-day basis and women's *bhajan mandalis* were held in public places.

Other than these religious activities, women also became part of groups that defied the state restriction on gathering of more than five people in public spaces. With agitation gaining intensity, people started defying the restriction and voluntarily getting arrested in the '*Jail Bharo* Movement'. For making this movement participatory, one day in the week was reserved for women coming forward to get arrested.

The participation of women in this agitation reflected a passionate sentiment among them. Bhatia notes that women were quite aggressive during the agitation. As she observes, women very often were seen,

> ...beating their chests, displaying swords and *trishuls*, and taking a pledge that they would keep the struggle going till the land is restored back to the Amarnath Shrine Board. They also chanted aggressive slogans like *lathi goli khayenge, zameen waapis layenge* (We will face guns and batons and get our land back); *Jammu ki naariyan, aag ki chingariyan* (Women of Jammu are like burning embers); *desh ke gadaron ko, jute maaro saalon ko* (Traitors to the nation should be beaten with shoes), *khoon bhi denge, jaan bhi denge, Bhole ki gaddi waapis lenge* (We will give our blood, we will give our lives too, but we will take back Shiva's (*Bhole*) throne).
>
> (Bhatia, 2009, 447-448)

One reason for massive participation of women in the agitation was that it was seen as a 'family affair'. Women joined in because their men were involved; they participated as part of the family of the men who were already agitating. It's not hard to guess if women would have participated had the men in their families not been part of the agitation. Since their men were already part of it, it was easy for them to join. Moreover, it was an extension of their daily religious chores.

In a way, participation in the agitation was just an extension of their role in the family that they were quite comfortable playing. Neither this was an exclusively women's affair nor were they raising any kind of women-related issues. Hence, their participation was not seen as contradictory to their day-to-day role. Most importantly, by participating, they were in no way stepping outside their designated role within the patriarchal society. They did not cross any 'gender-related' limit set for them within the structure of society.

Explaining this phenomenon, Bhatia notes that participation of women in such kind of politics 'is convenient for women in a patriarchal setting since it creates no dichotomy for them between their gender expectation and political orientation. Without contradicting the power structure, they can acquire activist roles (Bhatia, 2009, 450).' She further elaborates that,

> Generally, middle class modernity refashions the notion of 'femininity' in accordance with the contemporary processes of urbanisation, globalisation and homogenisation of urban cultures. The modern urban middle class woman is allowed to venture into the public or political sphere, pursue higher

> education, wear western attire and imbibe global consumerist values. Yet, this redefinition should not undermine the underlying 'womanly' virtues and certainly not threaten the basic pillars of patriarchy. Family and kin still remain the most essential spheres of influence that define the identity of the majority of urban woman. Rather than challenging oppression within these spheres and constructing their independent identity, women remain subordinated and dependent. The modern form of patriarchy in a consumerist culture provides new ways for women to be feminine, motherly and homemakers without interrogating the main issues of gender inequality and subjugation within and outside the family.
>
> (Bhatia, 2009, 448)

It was basically the religious nature of the agitation that brought large number of women to the public space. Although it had its regional connotations also, religious sentiments and religious response was the core point of the agitation, and women could very easily identify with it. As Ubbott notes,

> In a society, where very less public space is given to the women, temples hold an instrumental value for women to seek presence in public sphere. In the traditional set-up, women were mostly consigned to the homes and were subjected to stringent social norms, which were invariably patriarchal in nature. In such a situation, temples and the religious places (Ashrams) maintained by religious leaders (Gurus) provided legitimate entry points for women to enter

> public space. All activities and interactions carried by women at these places were considered to be within the limits of their gender roles.
>
> (Ubbott, 2010)

During the whole period of the agitation, religious activities being the major mode of protest, and also the participation of various religious personalities, had the effect of women getting associated with the agitation very smoothly. As one could see, the religious groups of women (*bhajan mandalis*), the religious heads of various sects (*gurus*) adopted by women, and the heads of various temples (*pandits*) had their share of role in mobilising women in the Amarnath agitation. In a way, they became the symbols of the religious identity of the community. They took the responsibility of 'carrying the cultural identity of Jammu on their shoulders and turned into the symbols of the community (Ubbott, 2010).' One can refer to Amrita Chhachhi's observation with reference to similar participation of women elsewhere. She notes that 'women become the symbols and repositories of communal/group/national identity and fundamentalism constructs notions of femininity and masculinity as symbolic of the community (Chhachhi, 1989, 162-163).'[56]

56 Amrita Chhachhi is a well-known scholar with an expertise on Gender and Globalisation. She has researched and written several books on gender, labour, poverty and socio-economic restructuring, citizenship, social protection and human security.

Though the participation of women in the agitation was mainly an urban phenomenon, the rural women also participated. What was peculiar about their participation was that it cut across the class-line; not only the middle-class women participated but also women of other classes. The Dalit women also participated in large numbers. However, the nature of their participation was quite different. For middle-class women, particularly lower middle-class women, it was more of a religious phenomenon and they used the strategies of holding *kirtans* and *bhajan mandalis* to show their support for the agitation. They would be singing along the beat of the *dholak*. The upper-class women coming from affluent areas mainly participated in peace marches. For educated and working women, it was a religious-cum-political event.

However, this is not to argue that women were participating in the agitation only for religious reasons. They shared with men the strong regional and nationalist sentiments. As all the debates, speeches and arguments regarding regional discrimination came up, they were overwhelmed by such feelings as well. In fact, the perception of regional discontent is pervasive among all classes of Jammu's society and women share this perception.

However, their participation did not in any case reflect their political autonomy, and gender, as a reason, never got any sort of reflection in this process of mobilisation. Neither personal nor political issues were seen from gender perspective. As stated above, they did not play any leadership role and did not cross any boundary set up by patriarchal norms. Even if they did participate intensely, they did not go against the expected gender norms. In fact, the way they participated in the agitation, the norms of sex-segregation were clearly reflected. With the agitation being led by men, women participating in it were mainly under the male supervision and male gaze (Bhatia, 2009).

With such massive participation of women in the agitation, one could expect some long-term implications for women. Their politicisation during the agitation however was not translated into their continued interest and participation in politics. The lone example of women gaining politically during the agitation was that of Shilpi Verma. Her husband had committed suicide during the agitation and she was seen as a symbol of the 'sacrifice' her husband had made for Jammu region. So she contested the 2008 Assembly election that took place immediately after the agitation. However, she could not win the election and her short political career ended with her defeat. However, as Bhatia has noted, Shilpi rather than representing an empowered woman, represented the typical patriarchal symbol of 'widowhood'. To quote her, 'Shilpi in many ways reflected the role that politicians had assigned to women during the agitation. Neither having an autonomous political role, nor an independent personal identity, she was merely a "martyr's wife/widow" (Bhatia, 2009, 450).' Ubbott also notes that Shilpi Verma was nowhere close to the image of an emancipated, empowered, political woman having an agency of her own. Essentially, she was used as a symbol of housewives, loyal to their husbands even after their death, to woo women voters (Ubbott, 2010).

To conclude, one can say that even if the women's participation in Amarnath agitation be pronounced political, the women, who fought for the political dignity of the region, neither claimed, nor got an independent political space for themselves in the region. The women of Hindu-dominated areas of the Jammu region participated in an overwhelming number in the Amarnath agitation, but very few women acquired leadership positions in it. Those few who did come in front were either elected representatives of the local government or women related to the male leaders of the different political parties in the region. There was no involvement of any women's organisation of the region in the agitation, nor did any woman leader emerge from it. On the contrary, many male leaders with no political background came into the limelight in the agitation. In fact, the SAYSS, which spearheaded the agitation, had no woman member in its executive committee, nor did it include any woman in its committee for negotiating with the government. Interestingly, even none of the government's representatives were women.

The women of Jammu region could not gain a fraction of political mileage out of the whole Amarnath agitation episode. Despite their huge presence in the agitation, the emergence of women's leadership, either in the movement or in its aftermath, was nowhere to be seen. Women's mobilisation for Amarnath was not translated into mobilisation for gender issues as no reference to gender issues within and outside, before and after the movement, took place. Women's visibility couldn't get translated into women's political strength. Large number of women symbolising the movement was not reflected in their political importance for political parties. No political party tried to woo women in the Assembly or parliamentary election immediately following the agitation. Women's issues didn't feature in political speeches of leaders of almost all political parties. For that matter, women's mobilisation did not result in greater number of woman winners in the elections or woman contestants or even woman voters in the region.[57]

57 In the state Assembly elections that took place barely a month after the agitation, a total of sixty-seven (67) women candidates tried their luck in seven phases of polling. A closer look at the Assembly elections reveals that three districts went to polls in the seventh and final phase of elections. Among them, the two districts of Jammu and Samba witnessed the maximum resistance during the Amarnath agitation and the third was Srinagar; and it is very interesting to note that the maximum number of women candidates i.e. thirty-one (31) were in fray in this phase only. At the same time, it is disheartening to note that not a single woman, from any party, could win the elections. All the three women, who won the Assembly elections in the state, hailed from Kashmir region. The BJP and Congress had fielded two women candidates each in Jammu region but all four lost.

Conclusion

Writing about women's role in the politics of Jammu and Kashmir is quite a difficult task mainly for two reasons. First, in the complex plural society of this erstwhile state, women don't form one homogenous group but multiple groups with different histories, different cultural patterns and altogether different political responses. The state as it existed from 1947 to 2019 was comprised of three different regions with each region having its own set of multiple and complex patterns of society. Though Kashmir region can be seen as the most homogenous region, even this region has had its very well-defined distinctions – the distinction between the Kashmiri Muslims and Pandits being the most important one. Jammu is much more complex; though the Dogra culture is predominantly seen here, it also hosts various other cultural zones – the Pahari-Pothwari, the Gujjar, the culture of Doda belt, etcetera. How plural the region is can be exemplified by simply highlighting the plurality of just one district – the Kishtwar district, where besides the religious diversity, there is linguistic-cultural diversity too. There are twenty-two spoken dialects in this district alone. Ladakh meanwhile has its own set of complex diversities.

How does one capture the question of women and politics in this complexity? It is an onerous task indeed!

Thus, being aware of this complexity and the difficulty thereby in handling the diversity of this erstwhile state, we have consciously restricted the scope of this book to the regional level of diversity and sought to cover the question of women's role in politics from the perspective of the three regions – Jammu, Kashmir and Ladakh. However, much of the focus of the book has been confined to the two larger regions of Jammu and Kashmir. Ladakh has been mostly mentioned in the chapter on electoral politics but there has been no detailed study of women's role or agency in any other context.

Second difficulty in exploring the question of women in politics of Jammu and Kashmir arises from the vast canvas of politics. Apart from the mainstream power politics, there has been the context of conflict politics and agitational politics. To understand the role of women in politics here, it is therefore important to locate women in this whole range of politics. It is from this perspective that the question of women has been explored from the angle of power politics, conflict politics and agitational politics.

It is due to the intricate scope of the book – both from the perspective of the multi-layered diversities in J&K as well as the multi-dimensionality of politics – that the subject has been restricted. An initial attempt has been made to draw a broad picture about the question of women in J&K and the location of women in politics. We hope that the huge gaps this study reveals will motivate others to undertake further studies in this area.

Women in Jammu and Kashmir, as we have seen in this study, have come a long way in empowering themselves. They now have greater exposure to the public spaces. In the last seven and a half decades, there has been a significant change in the scenario related to women. Compared to the situation before 1947, the number of women who are educated and employed is certainly larger and there is also a greater visibility of women in public spaces. In terms of their political role, we find they are coming out in large numbers to vote and to participate in public spaces – be it agitations, demonstrations or processions. In fact, as the study of conflict politics has shown, women as demonstrators have been the 'face' of this politics. In Kashmir specifically, they have been registering their visibility in the public spaces ever since the early 1950s. Another important factor about women in Kashmir has been their high level of political consciousness. In the context of conflict politics, women here have been highly politically mobilised and show a high level of political awareness.

And yet, it is paradoxical that their participation in the higher level of political roles is very restricted. Whether it is leadership position in conflict politics or decision-making position in power politics, women seem to be conspicuous by their absence. This picture of absence of women in the decision-making roles is common for all the regions of the erstwhile state. One can therefore say that patriarchal notions still intervene in the way women enter and rise in politics. For all practical purposes, women's lives are linked with familial roles and therefore their role in politics is also impacted by the traditional gender division of roles. With women's role being primarily defined by familial responsibilities, and the public space being seen mainly as the domain of men, women find it difficult to enter politics. As elsewhere in India, in Jammu and Kashmir also, familial route therefore is the easiest one for women to join politics.

Our study has shown another linkage of the family with women's participation in politics. Whenever one finds women located aggressively in politics – as in the case of protest demonstrations or agitational activities – it is mainly because such participation takes place at the family level. This is a kind of politics where there is involvement of the family as a unit and women find it very convenient to be active here. However, participation of women in such kind of politics rarely gets translated to women becoming politically empowered for a longer period, or women using this kind of politics for raising crucial gender questions.

One major reason for women in Jammu and Kashmir not having the capacity to fight patriarchal notions and claim their rightful position in politics is the absence of 'women's collective' in this erstwhile state. Women, rather than being bound by the gender identity, mostly locate themselves in one or the other broader cultural or political category. They see themselves as part of a religious/regional/cultural grouping rather than a part of the larger gender category of 'women'. Much of this is due to the fact that women's movement politics could never fructify in this state. With not much push from women themselves, the gender question in fact has remained in oblivion.

That is why though 'woman' as an issue remained central to much of the political narrative in J&K, particularly in Kashmir, yet the 'gender' dimension of women's identity remained invisible. Neither from the perspective of the state nor from the non-state actors was the question of 'woman' raised from the gender perspective. As women-specific politics does not take shape here, the question of women's empowerment has not been raised at any point of time.

As our study has shown, the gender identity is quite subordinated to the larger political identities and there have been lot of situations where the gender question has been subsumed by the question of these larger political identities. And in situations of conflict between gender identity and larger political identities, it is the larger political identity that is prioritised.

Further, due to the absence of women's movement politics and gender solidarity, there has been a clear-cut fragmentation of gender identity – with women being divided into different identity politics and taking contrary political and ideological positions.

Epilogue

The book *Silent Assertions: Women's Agency in Jammu and Kashmir Politics* took a long time in the process of drafting. Its layout was complete much before the structural changes took place in the state of J&K in 2019. In August 2019, when the special constitutional status was withdrawn by modifying Article 370 of the Indian Constitution, the state was also reorganised. It was bifurcated into two union territories – the UT of Jammu and Kashmir and the UT of Ladakh.

With the withdrawal of the special constitutional status under Article 370, the provision for restricted application of the Constitution of India and the Central laws to Jammu and Kashmir was substituted by a provision by which the whole Constitution of India was made applicable.

With the reorganisation of J&K, for the time being, the state has been downgraded to the status of union territory with the commitment that once the situation is normalised, the status of 'state' will be restored.

Much of the content of the book is based on the state of J&K before it was reorganised, and that is why Ladakh has been referred to as the third region of this state. Due to paucity of data and time, however, there is not much focus on Ladakh's politics and women in this book. We are conscious of the fact that Ladakh forms a major gap here. With this region now acquiring the status of union territory, it becomes all the more imperative to focus on this area. We may come up with a separate work on Ladakh in the times to come.

August 2019 changes notwithstanding, the role and position of women in the politics of Jammu and Kashmir remains the same. Much of our analysis about the political space occupied by women, though refers to the pre-2019 phase, continues to remain the same in the post-2019 period. Even so, we may refer to a few developments that have taken place during this post-reorganisation phase where the question of women has been raised or where women have been politically visible.

Interestingly, the question of women was central to the argument in favour of withdrawal of the special constitutional status of J&K State under Article 370 and special privileges under Article 35A. More specifically, it was Article 35A (which provided for protection of special privileges to the permanent residents of the state) which was seen as discriminatory to women.

While providing justification for withdrawal of the special constitutional status of J&K in the Parliament, an argument was made that Article 370 was discriminatory on the basis of gender, class, caste and place of origin. Special mention was made about the right of women to be treated equally along with men in terms of holding and inheriting property in case of their marriage outside the state.

Even before the withdrawal of Article 370, there was a contestation of Article 35A on the grounds of its being discriminatory towards women. It was argued that this Article specifically discriminates against the children of women who had spouses from outside the state. Even though the discriminatory practice of excluding women from the privileges enjoyed by the permanent residents of the state after they married outside the state was stopped after the High Court judgement against this practice in 2002, and these women now enjoyed full rights as permanent residents of the state along with men, yet the discrimination against the children of such women continued. While the spouse of a man marrying outside the state was legally treated as a permanent resident of the state and the children automatically got the status of permanent residents of the state, the spouse of a woman marrying outside the state was not given that legal status and the children were also not treated as permanent residents of the state.

With the repeal of Article 35A, the distinction being made between male and female spouses was no more relevant. However, the position was made quite clear after the provision for Permanent Resident status was substituted with the new Domicile Law. As per this law, introduced in 2021, the definition of a domicile was extended much beyond the scope of Permanent Residents. Besides those who were the permanent residents of J&K, the domiciles were to include a number of other categories of people – including various kinds of central government employees; those who have been the residents of the state for the past fifteen years; those who have passed their class X or class XII exams from J&K, etcetera. Later, as per an amendment in the Domicile Law, the spouses were included as a category eligible for getting the domicile certificate. The amendment made it clear that henceforth, for the spouses – male or female – it would be possible to get a domicile certificate merely on the condition that their partner is a domicile of J&K. Rather than extending this privilege to the 'wife' of the domicile, it was extended to the 'spouses'. With Tehsildar being identified as the authority for issuing the certificate, the required documents now include the domicile certificate of the spouse and the valid proof of marriage. With male spouses of women domiciles becoming eligible for being considered as a domicile of J&K, the discrimination faced by children of women married outside J&K has been resolved.

How have women responded to the context of post 2019 changes?

Though woman's question has been one of the central justifications for withdrawing the special constitutional status of Jammu and Kashmir, yet we do not find any gender-specific response to the political changes. As already stated, women do not form a collective or a political constituency. If they become vocal about this or any other gender-related issue, they do so as part of a particular identity politics – be it regional, tribal, caste or any other identity politics. They speak as Kashmiri Muslim women or Kashmiri Pandit women, Dogra/Jammu women, Ladakhi women or Gujjar women and so on, rather than as women. So it is difficult to draw a conclusion about their response to the changes as women.

One development related to politics and women in the post-2019 period however may be mentioned and that relates to the expansion of the Panchayati Raj Institutions via the third layer of Panchayats – the District Development Councils (DDC).

The DDC is a directly elected body comprising of fourteen members with a Chairman and Vice-Chairman elected by these members from among themselves. In all, there are twenty districts in the Union Territory, ten each in Jammu and Kashmir Division; and totally, there are 280 DDC constituencies, for which an eight-phased election was organised towards the end of 2020. What was significant about these elections vis-à-vis women, was the principle of reservation. Along with SCs and STs there was provision of 33% reservation for women, both at the level of members, as well as at the level of chairpersons. Of the ten districts of Kashmir, women were to be chairpersons in three districts (Baramulla, Ganderbal and Shopian), and similarly, of the ten districts of Jammu region, three districts were to have women as chairpersons (Kishtwar, Ramban and Poonch).

It is this principle of reservation that compelled the political parties to not only nominate more women as candidates but also mobilise women for votes. What was interesting about the election was that many young educated women filed their nomination papers, and every DDC reserved for women saw a keen competition among a number of women candidates. Despite the fact that many women candidates were fielded by male members merely because they could not contest elections, still one saw quite a few women leaders emerging out of this election. In all, 450 women candidates contested the election for 100 reserved seats.

That without reservation, it is not very easy for women to occupy political space as political representatives became clear from the fact that every district had the presence of women only through the process of reservation. Thus, with the exception of the district of Bandipora, every district had elected only five women DDC members (all from reserved constituencies). Bandipora was the only district which had six female members.

References

Ahmad, Mushtaq Ul Haq, 2011, 'Has Conflict Empowered Kashmiri Women', *Kashmir Dispatch*, Sept 9, http://www.kashmirdispatch.com/others/09095748-has- conflict-empowered-kashmiri-women.htm

Ali, Tariq, 2003, *The Clash of Fundamentalisms: Crusades, Jihads and Modernity*, Verso.

All Jammu and Kashmir National Conference, 1944, *Naya Kashmir,* National Conference Publication.

Alkire, Sabina, 2005, 'Subjective Quantitative Studies of Human Agency', *Social Indicators Research*, Vol. 74, No. 1 (Jan, 2005), pp. 217-260.

Anjum, Aaliya, 2011, 'The Militant in Her: Women and Resistance', *Al Jazeera*, August 2, https://www.aljazeera.com/news/2011/8/2/the-militant-in-her-women-and-resistance.

Ashcroft, Bill, Gareth Griffiths and Helen Tiffin, 2004, *Post-Colonial Studies: Key Concepts*, Routledge, London, 2004.

Bakhshi, Suneethi, 2009, *Kashmir: The History and Pandit Women's Struggle for Identity*, Vitasta.

Bazaz, Prem Nath, 1959, *Daughters of the Vitasta,* Pamposh Publications.

Bazaz, Prem Nath, 2011, *Daughters of the Vitasta: A History of Kashmiri Women from Early Times to Present Day*, Gulshan Publishers.

Bhat, Farooq Ahmad, 2015, 'Kashmiri Society as Reflected in Folk Literature: 1819-1947', PhD Thesis, University of Kashmir, Department of History.

Bhatia, Mohita, 2009, 'Women's Mobilisation in the Jammu Agitation: Religion, Caste, Community and Gender', *Economic and Political Weekly*, June 27, Vol. 44, Issue No. 26 &27, pp 447-448.

Bodha, Irm Jalali and Shabir Ahmad Sheikh, 2017, Identity of Women: A Socio-historical Study of Jammu and Kashmir (1846-1947), *International Journal on Arts, Management and Humanities*, 6 (1): 43-46 (2017).

Bose, Sumantra, 2003, *Kashmir: Roots of Conflict, Paths to Peace*, Sage.

Butalia, Urvashi, 2002, *Speaking Peace: Women's Voices from Kashmi*r, Publisher: Kali for Women.

Chhachhi, Amrita, 1989, 'Forced Identities: The State Communalism, Fundamentalism and Women in India' in D Kandiyoti (ed.) *Women Islam and the State*, MacMillan.

Chauhan, Neeraj, 2018, '500-woman unit to tackle J&K's female stone pelters', *Times of India*, July 2, https://timesofindia.indiatimes.com/india/500-woman-unit-to-tackle-jks-female-stone-pelters/articleshow/64820203.cms.

Chenoy, Anuradha M, 2002, *Militarism and Women in South Asia: Women and Civil Society*, New Delhi, Publisher: Kali for Women.

Choudhary, Zafar, 2012, *Locating Jammu Muslims in Kashmir Conflict: An Alternative Narrative of Kashmir Conflict*, Centre for Dialogue and Reconciliation.

Chowdhary, Rekha, 2016, *Jammu and Kashmir: Politics of Identity and Separatism*, Routledge.

Chowdhary, Rekha, 2015, 'Missing Girls in Jammu and Kashmir', *Daily Excelsior*, March 8.

Chowdhary, Rekha, (ed), 2010, *Identity Politics in Jammu and Kashmir*, Vitasta.

Cross Town News, 2019, 'Women Played Historic Role In 1978 During Poonch Movement: Panthers Party', December 8, https://www.crosstownnews.in/post/45534/-women-played-historic-role-in-1978-during-poonch-movement-panthers-party.html.

Dabla, Bashir A, 1991, *Working Women in Kashmir*, Rawat Publications.

Dabla, Bashir A, 2007, *Multi-Dimensional Problems of Women in Kashmir Valley*, Gyan Publishing House.

Dabla, Bashir A, 2014, *Domestic Violence Against Women in Kashmir Valley*, Publisher: Jay Kay Books.

Dabla, Bashir A, 2011, *Social Impact of Militancy in Kashmir*, Gyan Publishing House.

DasGupta, Sumona, 2001, *Breaking the Silence: Women and Kashmir,* WISCOMP.

Dewan, Ritu, 1994, 'Hamsheera, Humsaya Sisters, Neighbours-Women's Testimonies from Kashmir', *Economic and Political Weekly*, Vol. 29, Issue no. 41, 8 October.

Dhar, K. N., 1997, 'Lalleshwari: An Apostle of Human Values', in K. L. Kalla, *Eminent Personalities of Kashmir,* Discovery Publishing House.

Dhar, L. N., 1984, An Outline of the History of Kashmir in *Kashmir: The Crown of India*, Vivekananda Kendra.

Dhar, Sushant, 2015, 'Summers of Exile', in Siddhartha Gigoo and Varad Sharma (eds.), *A Long Dream of Home: The Persecution,*

Exodus and Exile of Kashmiri Pandits, Bloomsbury India, 73-88.

Dhar, Sushant, 2015, 'Life in the Camp', in Siddhartha Gigoo and Varad Sharma (eds.), *A Long Dream of Home: The Persecution, Exodus and Exile of Kashmiri Pandits*, Bloomsbury India, 133-140.

Dhingra, Rajni and Vaishali, Arora, 2005, 'At the Cross Roads: Families in Distress', *Journal of Human Ecology*, 17 (3), 217-222.

Dispatch Staff, 2018, Untitled, *The Dispatch*, April 13, https://www.thedispatch.in/26559-2

Drew, Frederick, 1980, *The Jummoo and Kashmir Territories: A Geographical Account*, Indus Publications.

Economic Times, 2018, 'Kashmir Government to raise Women Police Battalion to deal with Stone Pelters', July 14, https://economictimes.indiatimes.com/news/defence/kashmir-government-to-raise-women-police-battalion-to-deal-with-stone-pelters/articleshow/58398258.cms?from=mdr

EFSAS, 2020, '22 October 1947: The darkest day in the history of Jammu & Kashmir', European Foundation for South Asian Studies, October 16, https://www.efsas.org/commentaries/22-october-1947-the-darkest-day-in-the-history-of-jammu-and-kashmir/

Farooq, Omer, 2018, 'Divided by War, Reunited by Web: The Partition Saga of Two Rajouri Sisters', June 25, https://freepresskashmir.news/2018/06/25/divided-by-war-reunited-by-web-the-partition-saga-of-two-rajouri-sisters/.

Greater Kashmir, 2020, 'Two women injured in cross-LoC firing in J&K's Poonch' , November 21, https://www.greaterkashmir.com/news/latest-news/two-women-injured-in-cross-loc-firing-in-jks-poonch/.

Gupta, Bal, 2011, *Forgotten Atrocities: Memoir of a Survivor of the 1947 Partition of India*, Published by Bal K. Gupta.

Gupta, C. P., 2020, 'Recalling Mirpur Carnage'. *Daily Excelsior*, 22 November.

Hans, Asha, 2000, 'Women Across Borders in Kashmir: The Continuum of Violence', *Canadian Women's Studies*; Downsview, Winter, Vol. 19, Issue 4, 77-87.

Hans, Asha, 2000, 'Internally Displaced Women from Kashmir: The Role of UNHCR', SARWATCH, Vol. 2, No. 1, July.

Hoskote, Ranjit, 2013, *I, Lalla: The Poems of Lal Ded*, Penguin.

Indian Express, 2020, 'Woman injured as Pakistan Rangers shell areas along IB in Kathua', 19 November, https://www.newindianexpress.com/nation/2020/nov/19/woman-injured-as-pakistanrangers-shell-areas-along-ib-in-kathua-2225434.html.

Jaffrelot, Christophe, 2018, 'Ceasefire Violations in Kashmir: A War by Other Means?', Carnegie Endowment for International Peace, 24 October 2018.

Jamwal, Anuradha Bhasin and Shuchismita, 2012, 'Women's Voices in Jammu and Kashmir', *Journal of Borderland Studies*, Vol. 27, Issue 1, pp 95-104.

Jamwal, Anuradha Bhasin, 2010, 'Women's Identity and Politics in Jammu and Kashmir' in Rekha Chowdhary (ed), *Identity Politics in Jammu and Kashmir*, Vitasta Publishing.

Khan, Ilyas, 2017, 'Partition 70 years on: When tribal warriors invaded Kashmir', BBC News, North-west Pakistan, https://www.bbc.com/news/world-asia-41662588.

Khan, Nyla Ali, 2009. *Islam, Women and Violence in Kashmir: Between India and Pakistan*, Tulika Books.

Koul, Sudha, 2002, *The Tiger Ladies: A Memoir of Kashmir*, Beacon Press.

Kuttab, Eileen and Riham Barghouti, 2002, 'The Impact of Armed Conflict on Palestinian Women', http://home.birzeit.edu/wsi/images/stories/The_impact_of_armed_conflict.pdf.

Kashmir Life, 2022, J&K: The NFHS5 Results, June 3, https://

kashmirlife.net/jk-the-nhfs5-results-vol-14-issue-9-293330/.

Kazi, Seema, 2011, *In Kashmir: Gender, Militarization, and the Modern Nation-State,* South End Press.

Khajuria, Manu, 2018, 'A look at Jammu region where feminine power is worshipped', dailyO, https://www.dailyo.in/all/shakti-womens-day-goddess-mata-vaishno-dogra-jammu-and-kashmir-22729.

Kaur, Ravinderjit, 1996, *Political Awakening in Kashmir*, A P H Publishing.

Khan, Nyla Ali, 2014, *The Life of a Kashmiri Woman: Dialectic of Resistance and Accommodation*, Palgrave Pivot.

Khan, Farida Abdulla, 2005, 'Other Communities, Other Histories', in Zoya Hasan, Ritu Menon (ed), *The Diversity of Muslim Women's Lives in India*, Rutgers University Press.

Khurshid, Fouzia, 2011, 'Education and the Changing Status of Muslim Women: A Case Study of Srinagar District, Jammu and Kashmir', PhD Thesis, Aligarh Muslim University.

Mahjoor, Nayeema, 2016, *Lost in Terror*, Penguin Random House, India.

Malik, Inshah, 2018, *Muslim Women, Agency and Resistance Politics: The Case of Kashmir*, Palgrave Macmillan.

Malik, Inshah, 2010, 'Muslim Women in Kashmir: Family, Separatism and Militarization', Countercurrents.Org, April 12, http://www.countercurrents.org/malik120410.htm.

Malik, Inshah, 2013, 'The Muslim woman's struggle for justice', Seminar 643, March.

Manchanda, Rita, 2011, 'Kashmiri women demand participation in peace process', *Peace Talks*, February 4, http://peacetalks.hdcentre.org/2011/02/kashmiri-women-demand-participation-in-peace-process/.

Manchanda, Rita, 2001, 'Guns and Burqa: Women in the Kashmir Conflict', in Rita Manchanda (ed.) *Women, War and Peace in South Asia: Beyond Victimhood to Agency*, Sage Publications.

Manchanda, Rita (ed), *2001, Women, War and Peace in South Asia: Beyond Victimhood to Agency*, Sage Publications.

Manchanda, Rita, 1999, Kashmir's worse-off half', Himal, May 1, https://www.himalmag.com/kashmiraes-worse-off-half/.

Mann, R. S., 1978, 'Ladakhi Polyandry Reinterpreted', *Indian Anthropologist,* 8 (1), June, 17-30, http://www.jstor.org/stable/41919333.

Mehta, Krishna, 2006, *Kashmir 1947: A Survivor's Story*, Penguin Global.

Mishra, Shantanu, 2021, Inheritance Rights at bay: The story of Kashmiri half widows', *Law and Other Things*, February 11, https://lawandotherthings.com/2021/02/inheritance-rights-at-bay-the-story-of-kashmiri-half-widows/.

Misri, Krishna, 2010, 'Identity of Kashmiri Women', in Rekha Chowdhary (ed) *Identity Politics in Jammu and Kashmir*, Vitasta Publishing.

Misri, Krishna, 2013, Reminiscing an Era… 1947, *Kashmir Times*, December 5, http://www.kashmirtimes.in/newsdet.aspx?q=4341.

Moser, Caroline O.N. and Fiona C. Clark (eds.), 2005, *Victims, Perpetrators or Actors?: Gender, Armed Conflict and Political Violence*, Zed Books.

oneindia, 2006, 'Hindu Mother Unites with Muslim daughter after 57 years', June 24, https://www.oneindia.com/2006/06/24/hindu-mother-unites-muslim-daughter-57-yrs.html.

Parashar, Swati, 2014, *Women and Militant Wars: The Politics of Injury*, New York, Routledge.

Parashar, Swati, 2011, 'The Sacred and the Sacrilegious: Exploring

Woman's "Politics" and "Agency" in Radical Religious Movements in South Asia', *Totalitarian Movements and Political Religions*, 11: 3-4,435-455.

Ramachandran, Sudha, 'Dying to be Equal: Women Militants and Organizational Decision-Making', in Farah Faizal and Swarna Rajagopalan (eds.) *Women, Security, South Asia: A Clearing in the Thicket*, Sage Publications, New Delhi, 2005.

Ramachandran, Sudha and Sonia Jabbar, 2003, *Shades of Violence: Women and Kashmir,* WISCOMP.

Rai, Mridu, 2004, *Hindu Rulers, Muslim Subjects: Islam, Rights and the History of Kashmir,* Hurst & Company.

Ray, Ayesha, 2009, 'Kashmiri Women and the Politics of Identity', https://www.yumpu.com/en/document/read/12199585/the-kashmiri-woman-identity-and-politics-shur-luiss.

Samarasinghe, Vidyamali, 2012, '"A Theme Revisited"? The Impact of the Ethnic Conflict on Women and Politics in Sri Lanka', *Journal of Women, Politics & Policy*, Vol. 33, Issue 4, pp 345-364.

Saraf, Amar Nath, 2007, *Rajouri Remembered*, Published by Amar Nath Saraf.

Scroll.in, 2020, 'Jammu and Kashmir: 60-year-old woman killed in alleged cross-border firing in Poonch district', Scroll.in, July 08, https://scroll.in/latest/966833/jammu-and-kashmir-60-year-old-woman-killed-in-alleged-cross-border-firing-in-poonch-district0.

Shafi, Aneesa, 2002, *Working Women in Kashmir: Problems and Prospects*, APH Publishing.

Sharma, Ashutosh, 2019, 'J&K border residents in the line of India-Pakistan cross-fire', *National Herald*, 9 March, https://www.nationalheraldindia.com/india/jandk-border-residents-in-the-line-of-india-pakistan-cross-fire.

Sharma, Deepika, 2017, 'Social Welfare in the Princely State of

Jammu and Kashmir (1846 to 1947)', PhD Thesis, University of Jammu, Department of History.

Sharma, Deepika and Anita Rana, 2015, 'Social Evils Among Women in Jammu and Kashmir during Dogra Period and Colonialism and Reforms (1846-1925)', *IOSR Journal of Humanities and Social Science*, Vol. 20, Issue 3, Ver., VIII (March 2015) pp 08-20, 9).

Shekhawat, Seema, 2014, *Gender, Conflict and Peace in Kashmir: Invisible Stakeholders*, Cambridge University Press.

Shekhawat, Seema, 2006, *Conflict and Displacement in Jammu and Kashmir: The Gender Dimension*, Saksham Books International.

Snedden, Christopher, 2017, *Understanding Kashmir and Kashmiris*, Publisher: Speaking Tiger.

Sobhrajani, Manisha, 2008, 'Jammu and Kashmir: Women's Role in the Post-1989 Insurgency'. *Faultlines*: Volume 19, April 2008. http://www.satp.org/satporgtp/publication/faultlines/

State of Jammu and Kashmir ...vs Dr. Sushila Sawhney, 2002, October 7, https://indiankanoon.org/doc/1409240/).

Ubbott, Vibhuti, 2010, 'Gender Identity and Participation of Women in Amarnath Agitation', in Rekha Chowdhary (ed), *Identity Politics in Jammu and Kashmir*, Vitasta Publishing.

Vinayak, Ramesh, 2008, 'Dynasty's Own Women', *India Today*, November 15, https://www.indiatoday.in/web-exclusive/story/dynastys-own-women-33449-2008-11-15.

Vishav Raksha, 2005, 'Reflection of Family, Marriage and Gender in Dogri Folksongs', in S L Sharma, Satish K Sharma, Jayaram Panda, (eds), *Ethnic, Rural and Gender Issues in Contemporary North-West*, Anamika Publishers.

WaliKhanna, Charu, 2004, *Women, Silent Victims in Armed Conflict: An Area Study of Jammu & Kashmir, India*, Serials Publications.

Walter Roper, Lawrence 1895, *The Valley of Kashmir*.

Wazir, Rekha, 2019, 'The Women's Self Defence Corps, Srinagar 1947-48: A Conversation with Kanta Wazir'. *KashmirConnected*, http://www.kashmirconnected.com/articles--reports/category/womens-militia.

Whitehead, Andrew, 2021, 'For the Conversion of Kashmir: the massacre at St. Joseph's mission hospital in Baramulla' in Reeta Chowdhari Tremblay and Mohita Bhatia (eds) *Religion and Politics in Jammu and Kashmir*, Routledge.

Whitehead, Andrew, 2017, 'Kashmir's Forgotten Women's Militia', *The Wire*, October 23, https://thewire.in/gender/kashmir-women-militia.

Whitehead, Andrew, 2019, *The Lives of Freda: The Political, Spiritual and Personal Journeys of Freda Bedi*, Publisher: Speaking Tiger.

Whitehead, Andrew, 2007, 'Partition Voices: Mahmooda Ahmad Ali Shah and Sajida Zameer Ahmad', https://www.andrewwhitehead.net/partition-voices-mahmooda-ahmad-ali-shah--sajida-zameer-ahmad.html).

Women's Initiative, 1994, *Women's Testimonies from Kashmir: The Green of the Valley is Khaki*, Women's Initiative.

Yusuf, Shabir Ibn, 2021, '10% increase in crime against women in J&K, Ladakh: NCRB' Sept. 17, *Greater Kashmir*, https://www.greaterkashmir.com/todays-paper/front-page/10-increase-in-crime-against-women-in-jk-ladakh-ncrb.

Zia, Ather, 2007, 'Kashmiri women: Concerns, Milestones and Solutions'. Kashmir Affairs, http://www.kashmiraffairs.org/Zia_Ather_Kashmiri_women.html.

Index

A

Accession 27, 33, 39, 85, 93, 100

Agency vii, 9, 10, 11, 12, 13, 14, 32, 91, 105, 106, 141, 143, 145, 146, 165, 174, 197, 202

Agency of women 10, 11, 14, 105, 106

Agitational v, 178, 184

Agitational politics 12, 13, 57, 60, 178, 184, 202

Agitations 101, 178, 179, 180, 184, 185, 186, 187, 188, 189, 191, 203

Akbar Jehan 83, 84, 85

Anjuman-i-Nusrat-ul-Islam 23

Arya Samaj 23

Asiea Naqash 90

Assembly 41, 43, 61, 62, 63, 64, 65, 66, 69, 70, 71, 74, 75, 76, 77, 78, 79, 80, 81, 85, 86, 87, 89, 90, 92, 149, 197, 199

Assembly elections 65, 69, 70, 71, 74, 75, 80, 81, 86, 87, 92, 199

Awami National Conference 90

B

Baramulla 27, 45, 111, 115, 211, 222

BJP 71, 72, 73, 74, 75, 90, 136, 179, 199

Block Development Council 97

Bordering process 121

Border people 119, 122

Borders 100, 119, 121, 122, 124

Boycott politics 89

C

Campaign 43, 44, 48, 61, 65, 67, 165, 167, 174

Camps 55, 136, 137, 140, 151

Caste 95, 214

Ceasefire Line 107

Child marriage 19, 22, 23

Communist Party of India 36

Conflict politics vii, viii, 10, 11, 13, 14, 35, 36, 39, 60, 105, 142, 143, 144, 158, 162, 202, 203

Conflict situation vii, viii, 1, 10, 11, 13, 46, 66, 87, 100, 102, 103, 104, 105, 106, 127, 128, 129, 131, 135, 136, 142, 143, 145, 162

Congress 63, 64, 70, 72, 73, 74, 78, 86, 87, 91, 92, 149, 178, 179, 199

Constitution of Jammu and Kashmir 39

Contestants 12, 57, 70, 72, 73, 74, 78, 79, 80, 81, 199

D

Dalits 16, 117, 181

Dalit women 18, 196

Darakhshan Andrabi 90

Demonstrations viii, 48, 50, 52, 136, 148, 149, 150, 151, 161, 188, 203, 204

Discontent 48, 49, 64, 179, 180, 181, 182, 183, 184, 196

Displacement 11, 103, 124, 221

Divided families 118, 120, 125, 126

Division 29, 58, 70, 71, 95, 96, 107, 120, 123, 125, 126, 152, 163, 204

Dogra Rajput 17

Dogra Sadar Sabha 24

Domestic violence 29, 30, 135, 140

E

Educated women 28, 48, 172, 211

Education 22, 23, 24, 25, 26, 27, 28, 29, 33, 37, 39, 47, 48, 86, 91, 94, 103, 125, 130, 134, 158, 165, 167, 172, 173, 175, 176, 177, 194

Educational institutions 28, 160, 172, 184, 185, 189

Electoral politics 60, 61, 62, 63, 69, 83, 180, 202

Exodus of Kashmiri Pandits 101, 136, 137

F

Farooq Abdullah 84, 86, 90

Female infanticide 6, 19, 20, 22

Fencing 101, 122, 124

Folk 4, 6, 7, 8, 103, 114, 117

Freda Bedi 51, 222

Fundamentalist 10, 13, 165

G

Gender context of conflict 104

Gender identity 11, 12, 13, 14, 44, 46, 56, 204, 205

Gender question 14, 40, 205

Ghulam Mohammed Sadiq 85

Gujjars 15, 16, 35

Gujjar women 18, 210

H

Habba Khatoon 3, 4, 5, 6

Half widows 61, 129, 130, 145, 159, 219

Hijab 167, 169, 171

Hina Bhat 90

I

Identity politics 13, 35, 36, 40, 41, 46, 179, 181, 205, 210

Independent candidates 71, 74, 75, 77, 78

J

Jammu i, iii, vii, viii, 1, 6, 10, 11, 12, 13, 14, 15, 16, 17, 18, 19, 21, 22, 23, 24, 25, 26, 27, 28, 29, 31, 33, 34, 35, 36, 37, 39, 40, 41, 43, 44, 45, 47, 49, 50, 57, 60, 63, 65, 67, 68, 70, 71, 72, 73, 81, 83, 88, 90, 91, 92, 93, 95, 96, 97, 98, 100, 101, 102, 106, 107, 108, 109, 110, 111, 113, 114, 117, 119, 121, 126, 127, 128, 129, 136, 138, 161, 172, 178, 179, 180, 181, 182, 183, 184, 185, 187, 188, 190, 192, 195, 196, 197, 198, 199, 201, 202, 203, 204, 207, 208, 210, 211, 213, 214, 215, 216, 217, 218, 219, 220, 221, 222

Jammu region 6, 12, 15, 17, 18, 21, 23, 29, 49, 50, 57, 63, 65, 71, 81, 91, 92, 101, 107, 108, 109, 110, 114, 126, 178, 179, 180, 181, 182, 183, 184, 185, 187, 188, 190, 197, 198, 199, 211, 218

Janata Dal 78

Janata Party 63, 70, 78

JKNC 63, 64, 68, 72, 73, 74, 78, 86, 90, 149, 178, 179, 180, 181, 182

JKNPP 73, 74

K

Kashmir i, iii, vii, viii, 1, 2, 3, 4, 5, 6, 9, 10, 11, 12, 13, 14, 15, 16, 17, 18, 19, 20, 21, 22, 23, 25, 26, 27, 28, 29, 30, 31, 32, 33, 34, 35, 36, 37, 38, 39, 40, 41, 42, 43, 44, 45, 47, 48, 49, 50, 51, 52, 53, 55, 56, 57, 58, 60, 62, 63, 64, 65, 67, 68, 70, 71, 72, 73, 81, 83, 84, 85, 87, 88, 90, 91, 92, 93, 95, 96, 97, 98, 100, 101, 102, 106, 108, 110, 111, 113, 117, 119, 121, 122, 128, 129, 130, 132, 133, 135, 136, 137, 145, 146, 147, 148, 149, 150, 151, 152, 155, 156, 157, 158, 161, 162, 163, 164, 165, 170, 172, 173, 174, 175, 178, 179, 181, 182, 184, 185, 187, 188, 190, 199, 201, 202, 203, 204, 205, 207, 208, 210, 211, 213, 214, 215, 216, 217, 218, 219, 220, 221, 222

Kashmiri 2, 4, 5, 6, 9, 10, 11, 15, 16, 20, 21, 23, 29, 35, 40, 41, 42, 44, 48, 50, 53, 54, 58, 101, 130, 131, 132, 133, 134, 136, 137, 139, 150, 154, 155, 162, 166, 167, 170, 171, 172, 174, 178, 182, 188, 201, 210, 213, 214, 216, 218, 219, 220, 222

Kashmiri identity 35, 40, 41, 42, 44

Kashmiri Muslim 16, 21, 136, 137, 210

Kashmiri Muslim women 21, 136, 137, 210

Kashmiri Pandit 4, 10, 11, 136, 137, 139, 210

Kashmir region 15, 16, 20, 57, 62, 63, 64, 65, 81, 149, 179, 181, 182, 188, 199, 201

Khalida Shah 90

Kotli 23, 112, 119

Krishna Mehta 28, 82, 91, 92, 111, 114, 117

Krishna Misri 2, 25, 50, 52, 54, 58, 148

L

Ladakh 15, 16, 20, 29, 40, 49, 71, 72, 81, 83, 90, 91, 202, 207, 208, 222

Ladakhi 15, 210, 219

Lala Hans Raj 24

Lal Ded 3, 4, 5, 217

Land reform 180

Leadership viii, 10, 12, 24, 50, 51, 52, 58, 59, 99, 161, 163, 164, 168, 178, 179, 183, 186, 187, 188, 196, 198, 203

Legislative Council 43

legislators 57, 76, 82

Line of Control 107, 120, 121

Literacy 33, 50

M

Maharaja Gulab Singh 19, 22

Maharaja Hari Singh 24, 107

Maharaja Pratap Singh 24

Maharaja Ranbir Singh 22

Mainstream politics 12, 13, 44, 56, 57, 58, 89, 161, 162, 163, 166

Maqbool Sherwani 112

Mehbooba Mufti 68, 69, 72, 73, 74, 82, 83, 86, 87, 88, 162

Mehmooda Ahmed Ali Shah 28, 52, 85

Members of Legislature 12

Mian Rajput 17

Middle class 21, 28, 33, 47, 48, 150, 181, 193

Militancy 1, 60, 64, 65, 66, 71, 94, 101, 124, 134, 135, 136, 137, 147, 148, 151, 152, 153, 154, 155, 156, 157, 159, 165, 166, 168, 169, 170, 171, 173, 174, 175, 177

Militarisation 10, 101, 122, 135, 155, 156, 176

Mirpur 23, 24, 107, 109, 110, 112, 113, 216

Movements 220

Mufti Mohammed Sayeed 69

Muslim Conference 36, 47, 49, 108

Muslim United Front 63

N

National Conference 36, 37, 38, 39, 43, 47, 49, 50, 51, 52, 54, 63, 67, 71, 72, 78, 84, 85, 86, 90, 91, 93, 112, 113, 178, 180, 182, 183, 213

Naya Kashmir (New Kashmir Manifesto) 36

NFHS survey 31

Noor Gujri 51

P

Padma Sachdev 28

Paharis 15, 16, 35

Panchayati Raj Act of 1989 96

Panchayati Raj Institutions 46, 67, 93, 94, 211

Panthers Party 71, 72, 73, 187, 215

Patriarchal 7, 8, 10, 12, 16, 19, 20, 21, 41, 58, 59, 106, 131, 142, 145, 146, 193, 194, 196, 197, 204

Peace building 14, 144

Peace process 14, 106, 118, 119, 218

Peasantry 16, 47, 49, 180

People's Conference 63, 89

People's Democratic Party (PDP) 43

Permanent residents 38, 39, 41, 42, 44, 208, 209

PoK refugees 120, 127

Political identity 12, 13, 39, 40, 43, 44, 46, 61, 205

Political leaders 12, 57, 90, 91, 106, 166

Political mobilisation 40, 47, 56, 62, 63, 87

Politicisation of Women 146

Poonch 23, 35, 57, 65, 107, 109, 110, 112, 123, 185, 187, 211, 215, 216, 220

Position of women 6, 14, 16, 21, 32, 33, 67, 208

Praja Parishad 180, 182, 183, 188

Praja Parishad agitation 180, 183, 188

Processions 147, 148, 151, 189, 191, 192, 203

Prostitution 6, 21, 37

Protests 50, 64, 68, 132, 148, 149, 150, 157, 159, 160, 161, 178, 189, 191

Punjabis 23

R

Rajouri 26, 35, 45, 65, 71, 112, 113, 117, 216, 220

Rani Parvati Devi 83, 90, 91

Refugees 92, 109, 110, 120, 125, 126, 127

Regional identity 13, 35, 40, 179, 184, 187

Regional identity politics 13, 35, 179

Religion 10, 49, 119, 126, 152, 167

Religious diversity 15, 201

Religious identity 36, 47, 195

Reservation for women in Panchayats 96

Reserved constituencies 79, 80, 212

Resistance 7, 10, 11, 12, 56, 112, 113, 144, 149, 154, 165, 166, 171, 174, 178, 199, 213

Revivalist 13

S

Safina Baig 90

Sajad Lone 89

Sakina Ittoo 74, 86, 87, 88, 162

Sati 6, 19, 22

Scheduled Castes 95, 99

Scheduled Tribes 95, 99

Separatism 64, 148, 157

Separatist politics 10, 11, 12, 13, 14, 89, 101, 161, 162, 163, 164, 165, 174

Sex ratio 30, 45

Sexual violence 30, 32, 103, 115, 131, 132, 135, 156

Shabnam Lone 88, 89

Shanta Bharati 28, 92

Sheikh Abdullah 50, 51, 52, 59, 69, 83, 84, 90, 149

Sheikh Noor-ud-din Noorani 155

Shelling 101, 122, 123

Sub-regional identity politics 35

T

Tribal invasion 52, 85, 91, 100, 107, 108, 112

Tribal politics 35

U

University education 27

Urban local governance 97

V

Veil 16, 52, 165, 167, 169, 170

Veiling 17, 167, 168, 169, 171

Victimisation 10, 11, 13, 14, 106, 128, 132, 142, 143

Violence 9, 10, 106, 108, 113, 143, 215, 217, 219, 220

Violence against women 29, 32, 45, 102, 104, 139

Voter 62, 63, 64, 65, 66

Voter participation 62, 63

Voter turnout 63, 64, 65, 66

W

Widow remarriage 22, 23

Widows 61, 128, 129, 130, 145, 155, 159, 162, 219

Women candidates 69, 70, 71, 72, 73, 74, 76, 77, 78, 199, 211, 212

Women elite 28

Women party members 75

Women's agency 13, 106, 165

Women's employment 32

Women's militia 52, 53, 54, 55, 113

Women's movement politics 40, 205

Women's question 36, 45, 46, 88

Women's Voices 9, 214, 217

Working classes 49, 50